Dedicated to

My spouse,
Maggie Dodds Thompson.
We have a true storybook marriage.
She finds ways every day to strengthen our relationship.
She makes me a better person.
She helps keep me grounded.
She encourages me to soar to new heights.
Just by being, she makes the world a better place.
Without her love, patience and encouragement this book would never have come
to fruition.
Thank you, my love.

Acknowledgments

MANY HAVE HAD an influence on me and have helped shape this book but as in any endeavor some step up and do more than one could reasonably expect.

The first is Maggie to whom this book is dedicated. Her faith in me and trust that I could accomplish what I wanted to do framed my whole effort. She was diligent in editing every word I used. She not only helped me express myself in understandable words but also made sure even the most complex thoughts were stated more clearly than I originally penned. She was my "go to" person when I needed rescue from the idiosyncrasies of my computer. She speaks a digital language that stymies me daily. She produced my cover design. She patiently supported me when I experienced "writer's block" and gave me hope and determination to finish what I set out to do.

The second is Dr. William R. Allen, Professor Emeritus and past Chair of the UCLA Economics Department. He has authored many books on economics and contributed to many more. He was known as "The Midnight Economist," a syndicated radio program which helped his listeners understand complex issues that affected them directly. He stands in the company of other accomplished economists like Milton Friedman, Armen Alchian, James McGill Buchanan, Jr. and Joseph J. Spengler. Allen continues his influence through his writing and mentoring generations of students.

The next is The Right Reverend John Shelby Spong. Through his many books and meditations, he has become the major theological influence in my life. He has taught me to question and challenge every theological understanding I have. He opened the door to an infinite array of new possibilities when considering who or what God is like and how I can better play a part in God's creation. He has given me the courage to stand up and express my own theological musings even though they may challenge the understandings of others ... especially when they challenge the understandings of others. I cannot put a value on his kind words of encouragement and support, and I thank him for his words that appear on the cover of this book.

Another person who has had a major impact on me and the outcome of this book is Robert Burton who has taught the science of communication on the college level, drawing on his professional work in TV programming and technical production. He has a long tradition of free-lance presentations to community groups and organizations on a variety of topics of general interest. His awareness of how the public assimilates information has been most helpful and he has provided analysis and comment on the theological content of this book from a layperson's point-of-view.

Next, Dr. "Bob" Robert D. Thompson was instrumental with his encouragement. His specialty is psychological assessment strategy and measurement innovations in the world of business and government. His book, "Measuring the Unmeasurable," introduced him to others in his field. Bob is my brother and has a unique way of expressing himself professionally so that it is easily understood. He also has the gift of saying things simply and directly to me. He gave me the final push to author this book when I expressed my hesitation about writing something that could be controversial and unacceptable to many. His advice was "Just start writing." And so, I did.

There are three other persons who added valuable input. They are the Rev. Dr. Camilla Hempstead; Larry Bauer, a retired attorney; and Dr. Wendell Hess, Emeritus Professor and Chemistry Department Chair., Dean, Provost and Interim President of Illinois Wesleyan University. All three of them graciously read several of my chapters as I began the writing process. They offered invaluable comment on the content and the way it was expressed so that I became more confident I could communicate with those I intended to reach.

The Rev. Vaughn Hoffman and Jill Lutz, a good family friend, took it upon themselves to read the whole book to evaluate the writing and the book's content to give me an idea of the persons most likely to benefit from my words. Their reflections provided me with the direction I would follow to publication.

I have served under the guidance of several United Methodist Bishops. I wish to recognize one of them for his leadership. The

Reverend Bishop Woodie W. White has the unique ability to balance his commitment to the institution of the Church while at the same time finding a path through all the obligations of his position that enabled him to be a pastor in the truest sense to each of the churches and the ministers under his care. I am proud to have served in the Central Illinois Conference of the United Methodist Church under his tutelage [NOTE: His Episcopal Area is now identified as the Illinois Great Rivers Conference], and I have used him as a personal guide for my own ministry.

Over the years since my retirement, I have been privileged to have had three persons who are good preachers, teachers and pastors who are grounded with a solid theology and who carried out their responsibilities to their congregations with integrity. They took seriously the Word they were charged to preach and they demonstrated a true concern for those in their care. The first is the Rev. Richard (Dick) Petry, who served Jacksonville First UMC in Florida, as the Pastor of Visitation and Coordinator of Pastoral Care. Dick demonstrates through his life and ministry how to shepherd a congregation, and he enters the lives of those in his charge, helping them grow in their faith. The next is the Rev. Vaughn Hoffman, mentioned above, who serves as the Directing Pastor of Wesley UMC in Bloomington, IL. Vaughn communicates the gospel with a flair and style that refreshes and renews his congregation, sending them into the world as ambassadors of Christ. The third is the Rev. Dr. Wesley H. Wachob, Directing Minister of the Pensacola First UMC in Florida. A preacher of conviction, he has the unique talent of being able to express a sound theology in terms that are easily understood, providing his parishioners with what they need to be witnesses for Christ. It was good to be able to sit in the pew and reflect on the message each of these clergy shared. Their presence in the pulpit and in my life helped to form my theology.

My website is: http://focusontheology.com/. Beth Sennett wrote the code that brings it to you. You will find book information, random meditations, and a place where you can contact me. I appreciate the work she has done. I welcome your feedback and your following.

Cover photo by unknown author found at https://research.northumbria.ac.uk/support/2014/02/05/rd-funding-for-forensic-sciences-event/ licensed under CC BY-SA. Shadow image adapted from original photo.

Everyone loves a mystery, so I include my thanks to five other persons who have helped me through their friendship, encouragement and in practical ways to help me bring this book to fruition. Each of them preferred not to be given the credit they deserve but acted on my behalf because of our friendship. I thank each one of them.

Next, I wish to recognize my extended family. First, Keith and Olive Thompson who gave me to this world and who set the standards and desire for me to live a full and productive life. Maggie and I combined have five children. In order of birth they are: Dr. David Garrett Thompson, a member of the faculty at Illinois Central

College, who teaches history and who has written his own book, *The Norwegian Armed Forces and Defense Policy, 1905-1955*; Terry William Dodds, a successful and ethical private attorney (yes, they do exist); Wesley Everett Thompson, a contractor, potter, activist and one who has established an extremely small footprint, limiting his personal use of the earth's resources; Nora Jane Thompson, our only daughter, is a social worker for a private community agency serving the poor and oppressed in Cincinnati; and Geoffrey Brian Dodds, the Municipal Attorney and City Manager of Heyworth, Illinois. They all are concerned about the betterment of others. Together they have nine children, who my mother would have said, "They are beautiful and each one is a genius." Thank goodness grandmothers and great-grandmothers are never biased.

As you read this book you will find that the author believes that the experiences and relationships we have with others determines in large part the theological understandings and positions we hold in society. All those mentioned above and the people making up each of the congregations I have served are responsible in large part for at least some of the theological ideas expressed in these pages. I am happy to have shared in the life of the following congregations: Fairview and New Zion UMC's in Baltimore, OH; Croton UMC in Croton, OH; Hebron UMC in Hebron, OH; Morton UMC in Morton, IL; Silvis UMC in Silvis, IL; Peter Cartwright UMC (and Methodist Historic Shrine) in Pleasant Plains, IL; Ritchy UMC and Wilmington First Presbyterian Church in Wilmington, IL; McLean and Waynesville UMC's in McLean and Waynesville, IL and Wesley UMC in Bloomington, IL (retired staff). The people of each of these churches and communities and those with whom I worked and served as a chaplain at the Methodist Medical Center in Peoria, IL all helped me to grow spiritually.

I am grateful to one other minister, the Rev. David Gaffron. He was my pastor in Bloomington, IL when I suddenly lost my vision. None of the doctors we contacted in Central Illinois held out hope for me but David gently insisted that my wife search and research the internet to see if we could find some help. Because of his suggestion, we found the next person I wish to recognize.

A special thank you goes to Harry W. Flynn Jr., M.D., the J. Donald M. Gases Distinguished Chair in Ophthalmology at the University of Miami, Miller School of Medicine. He is Professor of Ophthalmology at the Bascom Palmer Eye Institute and specializes in medical and surgical treatment of diseases of the retina and vitreous. In 1998 my eyes hemorrhaged due to complications of diabetes. He has given me nineteen years of eyesight. Through his pioneering surgeries and experimental treatments, he has restored my vision to 20/25. Without his talent and dedication to his patients and profession this book would not have been written.

Table of Contents

We need a map to plan our route. We must collect provisions so we are prepared for the unseen and unknown pitfalls we may encounter. We need to gather guides who already have walked the territory we plan to explore. We need to be willing to rely on others who have something to contribute to our common safety and on whom we can count to see us through to the end of our pilgrimage. You will find that the first two chapters provide these things.

Once we have made our preparations and are comfortable with our plans and the abilities of our guides, we are ready to venture into the unknown. This book concentrates on the way Christianity developed and spread but the same principles and process can be used to explore any faith expression.

Our faith exploration does not center on ourselves. It centers on our vision of what God may be like. Traditionally, the Christian views the divine being we call God as having three distinct, but interwoven, features. We call this the "Holy Trinity." "Father, Son, and Holy Spirit." "Creator, Redeemer and Sustainer."

Chapters Three, Four and Five deal with the Trinity in a new way ... a way that updates our religious understanding so it reflects twenty-first century thought. SPOILER ALERT! Read each chapter in its turn. Do not jump to these three chapters before you have read the first two. If you do so, you will not be prepared sufficiently to see this exciting journey to the end. You cannot go back and read the first two chapters and have the same understanding that will come from taking the journey in proper sequence. I realize that by having issued this warning there is great temptation to do just what I warned against, but if you yield to this temptation, you will be cheating yourself from gaining as much from your journey as you could have gained.

Each of the remaining chapters deal with specific religious topics. First, you will examine the role of Prayer and see the influence it has on the way we form our religious thought. Second, you will discover how the idea of Sin helps to shape our core ideas about religion. Next, you will explore the difference between Sin and the Nature of Good and Evil and find that this difference gives you freedom to challenge or affirm your religious understandings. The chapter on Eternal Life opens new possibilities for living in the present in a new way. The chapter on Worship allows you to see how different liturgical styles can bring us together rather than causing a separation between believers. And finally, the last chapter encourages us to read Scripture like a detective might read the clues left at the scene of a crime, so you can gain insight into the message God has for us.

I welcome you to journey with me. I do so with the knowledge that each of you has some insight that I may not have. So, in the end, when you have finished reading and thinking about what I have had to say, I encourage you to contact me and to share your thoughts because together we can come closer to the hope God has for this world and everyone who inhabits it. You will find ways to contact me at the end of this book.

Peace,
J. Allen Thompson

Part One

The Past

Premise of Chapter One:

An analysis of most religions reveals a similar pattern in their growth and faith development.

CHAPTER 1

"In the Beginning ... God"

I HAVE A story to tell. It's a simple story of the beginning of religion for an ancient people. But, more important, it is the story of the beginning of your religion and mine. [NOTE: This story is an example of what an adherent of the Phenomenology of Religion might use to explain the origin of religion. An explanation of the Phenomenology of Religion follows the story.]

Abougli [Aah-boo-glee] lived long ago in a land far, far away. He was short in stature, the "runt" of the litter. Because of his size he couldn't keep up with the hunters of the tribe when they went out to get food. So Abougli stayed with the women and children while the other men were foraging. There are hunters ... and there are gatherers. Abougli was destined to be a gatherer.

As a gatherer, Abougli was to labor, finding firewood and tall grasses for thatch, cutting small limbs and trees to be supports for sheltering roofs; hauling rocks for fire pits; and trekking long distances to the nearest source of water for drinking, cooking, and making medicines. It was this last task that Abougli liked best. It was hard work and lonely at times, for water sources weren't always nearby. It would take the better part of a day to get to the river and back, balancing one pot on his head and carrying two more pots, one at each end of a branch supported by his shoulders.

Sometimes Abougli wondered why his tribe had settled so far from the river, but he knew the answer. The men had to travel just as far in the other direction into the hill country to their hunting grounds. Living on the plain, halfway between their water source and good hunting seemed fair.

Abougli thought about many things as he trekked to the river and back. He marveled at the way birds soared over his head. He scurried past the place he had seen snakes and lizards so many times. Why were they so different? Snakes had no legs, and lizards were just plain frightening. He wondered about the flat rocks near the river. They seemed so hot on bright, sunny days. Where did the wind come from and where did it go? The life Abougli led had so many questions and so few answers, but he was happy, living with his tribe and finding his place in the scheme of things.

One day, as Abougli was walking back to his village with his load of precious water, a bird swooped low over his head. It commanded his attention and he followed its flight. He wasn't concentrating on the path, and he stumbled on a root that had grown up thru the dirt. Much of Abougli's water was lost. It was too late in the day to go back, so Abougli had to return home. It was not a good day.

When he arrived at the village, he had to tell what had happened. He was ashamed, and he knew his clumsiness had brought hardship to his friends. As he told his story over and over to those he met, something strange came about. Two of the older women who had fetched water in the past told Abougli that they, too, had stumbled in nearly the same place. They, too, had been distracted from the path.

The next day Abougli gathered his pots and went on his way. In the place he had stumbled, Abougli looked around. The root that had caused the accident was there all right, but it seemed so small ... hardly big enough to make him fall; but Abougli couldn't stay long. He had work to do. He went on, filled his pots, and began his journey home.

As Abougli neared the accident site, he was especially careful. He stepped over the root and took a few more steps. Then, he turned around to look at the root and sighed in relief. He had made it. As he turned back, he stepped on an especially sharp rock, twisting his ankle. Down he went again! What was there about this place? Again, Abougli returned to his village with little water and much shame.

The villagers couldn't believe it! Was Abougli getting too old to carry his load? Was he just plain clumsy? Didn't he care? It was decided that tomorrow one of the old women who had fetched water before would go with Abougli, and together they would get a double measure of water. They were in dire need of the precious fluid.

Together, they set out. Together, they looked at the spot where Abougli had fallen. There was the root. And there was the rock. They walked on in silence. After filling their pots with water, they started back. Abougli took the lead, and the woman followed, struggling under her load. They came to the PLACE.

Abougli carefully made his way past the root and the jutting rock. When he got past the obstacles, he turned around to check on the progress of his companion. There she was, hurrying to catch up. Just as she got to the place, something rustled in the grass near the path, and it startled the woman. She slipped to one knee, howling in pain, and her water splashed all over the ground!

She couldn't walk without help, and the day was going fast. Abougli had no choice but to leave his pots and help the woman back to the village. When they arrived without their treasure, everyone gathered to find out what had happened. Abougli and the woman told their tale, and the tribe reacted much as you would expect. Some were angry ... others were puzzled. Some were sympathetic, while others threw blame. It was a free-for-all. Finally, when things began to calm, someone suggested that perhaps the gods were angry. Maybe this place was a Holy place and none of them had any right to be there.

That idea made sense. How else could anyone explain it? So, they devised a plan. The next day they would all go to the site and see what they could see. Abougli and the woman led the tribe. Men, women, and children followed with excited words. As they approached the site, a hush came over them. Each one of them felt the power of this place. It WAS Holy!

The leader of the tribe knew what to do. After all, he was very wise. He told the villagers to spread out and gather some rocks … big rocks … rocks that were grand enough to build a pillar. That was it! They would build a monument to the gods, which was worthy of their power and mystery. And so, they did!

⟴≡◉ ◉≡⟴

Choices made by any individual determine how and where that individual fits into society. The study of how these choices impact the individual and society in general is known as phenomenology. Philosophers who subscribe to a phenomenological approach have a logical and formal way of dissecting societal influences so they can be analyzed with a limited amount of of bias. The basic question that the phenomenology of religion tries to answer is, "What is religion?" When a phenomenological approach is applied to the study of religion, no favor can be given to any faith persuasion. For this reason, the Church has decried the phenomenological method, because the Church cannot separate itself from its own biased understandings of itself. [NOTE: References in this book using the word "church" will have three distinct connotations. When the word has a lower case "c," "church" refers to the church universal and is not meant to reference any denomination or branch of Christianity. When the word has an upper case "C," "Church" refers to the Roman Catholic arm of Christianity, prior to the Schism, beginning in 1054 A.D. and continuing to 1453 A.D. and the Reformation, starting in 1517 A.D. When the word has an upper case "C," "Church" can refer also to either the Roman Catholic arm, or the Eastern Orthodox branch, or the Protestant divisions of Christianity after the "Great Schism" and the Reformation.]

Phenomenological philosophy applied to the study of religion began to be postulated toward the end of the nineteenth century. Prior to this, religion was examined from the bias of the believer. This new philosophy stretched the boundaries of classical philosophy by developing the idea that religions came about in much the same way as other societal influences. Religion, like other aspects of society, was analyzed from outside the influence of religion itself.

Religion was treated as a distinct societal influence separate from historical, societal, anthropological, philosophical and theological approaches to the study of religion. Unlike them, it treats religion as a phenomenon that cannot be explained in terms of any particular aspect of human society, culture, or thought—e.g., as the product of history, as a creation of intellectual elites, or as a set of truth claims about reality or the ends of human life—though it interacts with all of these aspects. [NOTE: Matt Stefon. "phenomenology of religion". **Encyclopedia Britannica. Encyclopedia Britannica Online.** *Encyclopedia Britannica Inc., 2012.]*

It is no wonder that the Church fought this phenomenological approach. It was an approach that seemed to be a threat to its very existence. If logic and reason were to be the criteria for examining faith, how could the Church maintain its status? The Church had long maintained that faith is defined as believing in something that can't be proved. That simple idea was the answer the Church provided when its authority over questions of faith was challenged. Though simple, it was a defense that has thwarted a huge variety of challenges over the centuries.

Phenomenological philosophers gained in stature. As they looked at the major world religions, they concluded that especially the Christian, Jewish, and Islamic faiths had a commonality that the other major religions did not have. They determined that the monotheistic belief of these three religions was the starting point for their examination. These secular philosophers found each of these three faiths woven with a similar thread that determined their development.

One of the first things they found was that for the person who grows up in a society composed mainly of Christians, the religion that person most likely would adopt is Christianity. Those growing up in a Jewish community most commonly would follow Judaism; and those who were raised in an Islamic community most probably would become Muslim. Any person tends to choose to be of the same faith as those who are most influential in his life.

There are exceptions. They occur when a person is not only a member of a major social group but is also a member of a sub-group.

For example, a person born in one of Brooklyn's neighborhoods where a large Jewish population resides may choose to claim the Jewish faith even though most of the population in Brooklyn is Christian. Personal relationships can outweigh the general experiences of most of the population.

While the social-psychological dynamic dominates the decision, not everyone in any given society will adopt the majority faith. This is especially true in the United States. A part of our heritage is that we are a society of many cultures and religions. It is estimated that in New York City inhabitants speak hundreds of different languages. We are the "melting pot" nation, giving meaning to our claim of being a free society where the individual can make the choices most relevant to his own background and situation. [NOTE: April 29, 2010. The New York Times. "While there is no precise count, some experts believe New York is home to as many as 800 languages — far more than the 176 languages spoken by students in the city's public schools or the 138 languages that residents of Queens, New York speak, that borough being the most [ethnically] diverse borough as listed on their 2000 census forms."]

The story of Abougli and his experience fetching water tells of the beginning of organized religion for this ancient tribe. Until the moment the chief told his followers to gather stones and build a pillar to honor the gods, the tribe had no definable religion. They knew there was a power and forces in the world that were greater than anything they could claim, but no one was able to define that power. It took a special event and a special place to begin to identify the god-force they felt had control over their lives. When this happened, they had to honor that mysterious force by setting aside a holy place for that power to dwell.

Stories like the story of Abougli have been repeated over and over to different peoples in different lands. The first common thread all these people had in the establishment of their religion was that they knew there was a power beyond themselves that was a determinate for their lives. That common thread still exists in our world, and is part of our faith development.

The truth and importance of this simple story insults many who participate in an organized religion today. The proponents of the phenomenology of religion maintain that though the story seems simple, it provides a major revelation as to the way present religions have developed. To others, it seems implausible that something so simple and far removed from our life experience could be the start of the sophisticated faith we hold in our time.

The proof comes as we take away some of the mystery of faith by linking religion with the psychology of community and social group interaction. We seek answers to the unanswerable. "Why me?" we ask. "What or who is God?" "Who are we?" "How can we get beyond ourselves to the really important things of life?"

The story of Abougli tells more than a tale of a long-ago tribe. It tells of the way religion takes root in the imaginations and minds of people in all ages. The way to best explain some things is to attribute the mystery of the unknowable and unknown to a power that is beyond us. Again, and again in different places to different people, the answers to the mysteries of life have been explained by developing a god-image that is more powerful than anything any human could possess. Because this god-image is so far removed from human limitations, it must reside in the realm of the spiritual. As we seek answers, some find demons and devils; some find witches; some find saints and servants; some don't find anything at all. But, some find God.

The human psyche is a wondrous thing. Based on our own individual experiences and relationships, we come to a variety of conclusions about almost everything. That is why we have good people who align themselves at opposite ends of the political spectrum. That is why we have good people who identify themselves as "pro-choice" or who become "right-to-life" proponents. That is why we have good people who are "peaceniks" or who are "war-hawks." Some favor capital punishment, while others abhor it. Almost anything can be seen as a legitimate option, when viewed from different vantage points. People see things differently because of their unique experiences and relationships. That single fact in large part determines who we are.

The differences one person has in his spiritual understandings and religious practices from another person's spiritual understandings and religious practices are determined in a similar way. As with ethical issues, dealing with religious issues yields myriad viewpoints. Both our ethical and religious views are in large part determined by the things we have experienced and the people around us. Our collective experiences and others to whom we gravitate have a profound influence on how we interpret the great questions of life.

Remember Abougli. The strange things that happened to him didn't make sense until the whole tribe felt the mystery and power of the place where he and others had fallen. Their collective experience gave credence to the idea that they were in a holy place; and they set about to mark it with a pillar of stone, so all would know about the power that resided there.

In the twenty-eighth chapter of Genesis, verses 10-22, we find the story of Jacob's dream at Bethel. This sacred scripture for both the Jewish and Christian communities tells a story much like the story of Abougli. Earlier in Genesis, we learn of God's blessing on Abraham for his willingness to sacrifice his only son, Isaac. God promised that Abraham's offspring would be plentiful and would become God's people; and after Abraham's death God blessed Isaac, as well. God's people were to be the people of Abraham and Isaac.

Isaac's sons, Esau and Jacob, were to benefit from God's continued blessing. But Jacob cheated Esau, the firstborn of Isaac, out of his birthright. In doing so, Jacob became the one upon whom the fate of God's people rested. Esau was furious for having been cheated, even though he had been willing to give up his birthright for his immediate needs earlier in the story. To escape Esau's wrath, Jacob fled and hid in a cave. Worn out and afraid, he slept on the ground with a stone for a pillow.

He dreamed that he, like Abraham and Isaac, would be blessed by God and given protection so that God's people could prosper in a land of their own. When he awoke, Jacob knew that God dwelt in this place. So, he took the stone upon which he had rested his head and poured oil on it and set it as a pillar to mark the spot, and he made his covenant (or agreement) with God. The names have been changed and the events have been altered, but like Abougli, Jacob marked the place he understood God to dwell.

You have only to look around to see our modern-day "pillars of stone" that mark our own holy places. They are monuments to our differing explanations of the religious questions of life. We may be more sophisticated than Abougli's clan, but in a real sense, our holy places have come about by the collective experiences of others through the centuries.

The story of Abougli tells of the first of our religious ancestors. Others have followed. For the Christian, they include Abraham, Isaac, and Jacob. They include other men and women of importance to those of the Jewish faith. They include Mary and Joseph. Our ancestors have gone by the names of the disciples, including Judas. They include the apostle Paul and the evangelists we call by the names of Matthew, Mark, Luke, and John.

Our family tree includes the leaders of the Roman Catholic Church and those who moved to reform it. We have ancestors in our Christian family tree from branch religious groups like the Greek, Romanian, and Russian Orthodox Churches. We must include even groups "outside" normal consideration because of their hateful and restrictive approach toward others; but we are required to do so because of their claim to be Christian. These groups will be discussed later, but for now we must consider the title "Christian" as being extended to all who identify themselves as being so.

Throughout the centuries there have been many who have helped form the Christian faith: Ignatius of Antioch who dealt with the practical matters of the Church (e.g., how the church related to Jesus, the role of the Sacraments, and the establishment of a fundamental church hierarchy); and Clement of Rome, aka Pope Clement I, who was consecrated by Saint Peter as a Bishop of Rome, are the first two worth noting.

Our ancestors include the great religious theologians of each century who gave form to our faith. They include those who were triumphant in their endeavors to define the Church and those who lost that battle. We will deal with some of them in the next chapter, but now we need to look at how some of our religious understandings came about.

There is no modern-day religion that can stand alone, separate from other religions. We need to compare other faiths to our own to provide a framework for our own understandings. No religion can claim to be unique from its inception. Even though the Christian claims Jesus as being unique to his religion, Christianity draws its identity from Judaic influences. We have a commonality with our

Jewish brothers and sisters. Jesus may be seen as our unique "possession," but the life and teaching of Jesus is rooted in the Jewish faith. We also have adopted the Judaic concept of a monotheistic God.

Over the centuries a distinction has been made between the Christian and Jewish faiths based on the concept of salvation. The Christian claims that salvation comes through the sacrifice of Jesus on the Cross. The Jew claims that salvation comes from faithful adherence to Judaic Law. As time has passed, the Christian Church has compromised its understanding. It still proclaims that salvation comes from the acceptance of Jesus as the Christ who died as a sacrifice for our sin. But the Church has tempered the concept of salvation with the idea that living a "right" life pleases God and provides us with the forgiveness of God. In other words, if we live by the law of good conduct, we will be "saved." "Faith cannot be separated from good works" is the banner under which the two become entwined.

Islam, too, has a common tie to Christianity. Muslims also claim one God and have a common history with Christians and those of the Jewish faith. Daily prayer rituals may seem foreign to a Christian and be more reflective of those of the Jewish faith, who have a prayer for almost everything; but there is more to Islam than that. All three religions trace their beginnings back to Abraham. In addition, each religion has a person through whom the faithful can embrace God. For the Christian, that person is Jesus. For those who are Jewish, that person is Moses. For the Muslim, that person is Mohamed. All three faiths have a person who is seen as having revealed the true nature of God and how we are to respond to God.

If the faithful of any of these three religions truly believe there is only one God, who has created everything and everyone, how can they dare rip from God all those who worship under a different name? God has created the Christian, the Jew, and the Muslim. All peoples belong to God. God has provided the experiences others have had. God has provided everyone with the ability to see God, as God wants to be seen. The force we call God makes itself known to different persons in different ways. How can any faithful person dare put himself in a position to judge the way other persons become believers? When this happens, it is a judgment about the faith of others <u>and</u> a judgment about the will of God.

Furthermore, a part of the development of religion depends on how the faithful can answer the questions of life that confront them. "Is God judgmental?" "Is God just?" "Does God love and forgive?" How we answer these questions depends on how God has been pictured through the ages. For Christians and for Jews, the first eleven chapters of Genesis describe God's nature and reveal how God's children should try to relate to each other and to God. These eleven chapters contain the stories of Adam and Eve, Cain and Able, Noah and the flood, and the Tower of Babel. Later, we will go into detail about some of these chapters, but here we deal with the story of Noah.

We hold scripture to be sacred because it sheds light on God's nature and the call that is placed on our lives. It is the job of scripture to reveal the answers we seek as we try to make sense of life. In the story of Noah, we learn of the evil side of human nature. The society of which Noah was a part was totally corrupt. In Noah, we find a man who was not only righteous and just, but a man who was willing to risk everything to do what he felt God wanted him to do.

We, too, can get battered about in the turmoil of life and the floods of circumstance. Life can simply overwhelm us. When it does, we are like Noah, riding out the storm. When the storm clouds dissipate and the flood of despair begins to recede, we once again can see God as having compassion. We can see God as the One who is willing to forgive and provide us with another chance at life. That is the simple but great message of Noah and the flood.

But, the Bible isn't the only source of a flood story in religion. It is common in the religious development of the American Indians to find such stories. It is a common theme in other religions, as well. Even before the story of Noah was written there was another version of the flood that parallels in many ways our story in the Bible. It is called *"The Epic of Gilgamesh."*

The **Epic of Gilgamesh** *is an epic poem from Babylonia and arguably is the oldest known work of literature. The story includes a series of legends and poems integrated into a longer Akkadian epic about the hero-king Gilgamesh of Uruk (Erech, in the Bible), a ruler of the third millennium B.C.E. Several versions have survived, the most complete being preserved on eleven clay tablets in the library of the seventh-century B.C.E. Assyrian king Ashurbanipal.*

The essential story tells of the spiritual maturation of the heroic Gilgamesh, the powerful but self-centered king who tyrannizes his people and even disregards the gods. He is part divine and part human. Through his adventures, Gilgamesh first begins to know himself through experiencing the death of his only friend, Enkidu. Seeing the secret of eternal life, he travels on the archetypal hero's journey, ultimately returning to Uruk a much wiser man than when he left and reconciled to his mortality.

The Epic appears to have been widely known in ancient times and to have influenced important works of literature, from the book of **Genesis** *to* **The Odyssey.** *One of the stories included in the epic directly parallels the Story of Noah's Flood.* [NOTE: **"Gilgamesh, Epic of." New World Encyclopedia. 8 Sep 2008, 12:03 UTC. 8 Jun 2012, 11:50.** *http://www.newworldencyclopedia.org/p/index.php?title=Gilgamesh,_Epic_of&oldid=802135>.]*

The Epic is an attempt to answer a variety of questions about life. As in the case of Abougli, when things seem unanswerable, they are attributed to a greater power or powers. In the Epic, there is a flood story that tells of the gods, who unleash a mighty flood to destroy humankind. There is one god who foils their plan and warns one person of the impending doom. The man is told to tear down his house and use the wood to build an ark. Being faithful, the man gathers his family and some workers, and they begin construction on a gigantic ark. When the man's neighbors question him, he tells them he has lost favor with the gods and is going to move, but they don't have to be afraid, because they will be rewarded.

The ark is completed just in time, and the man takes on board his family, some workers, and a variety of animals to protect their kind. He then seals the ark from the elements, and they ride out the storm. Waters are unleashed, the skies darken, and the winds howl. The storm is of such magnitude that even the gods cringe and hover in awe at the might of the power they have unleashed.

Finally, as in the biblical flood story, the ark is grounded, but as far as one could see, the waters had not abated. So, the man releases birds, one at a time, until finally the bird does not return. The man then knows that it is safe to disembark for there is land enough to provide vegetation. They leave the ark and build a monument to show thanks to the gods.

The purpose of referring to *The* Epic is not to minimize the biblical flood story, but to point out that religion, ancient and modern, has a way of developing along similar lines. When we try to answer the unanswerable, sometimes the only answers come when we attribute things to powers beyond ourselves.

Finding an earlier version of our flood story doesn't take from it the lessons it offers. It is a recognition that what turned out to be important to early Christians and earlier Jews was also important to an even earlier community. The human condition and how humans relate to God is a universal force that has existed through the ages. That force has continued, as evidenced by the flood stories in Native American Indian cultures. We are not unique in our need for answers of how God operates in the world, or how we are to relate to each other and to the divine image we have conjured up in our religious expressions.

It does not matter if the flood story long cherished by Christians has been adopted from the Jewish faith story, or if it comes from ancient Babylonia. It does not matter if it happened at all. In fact, a majority of modern biblical scholars do not believe that it did happen. Most main-line Christian seminaries maintain the Flood Story is one of several allegories presented in the early chapters of Genesis. It is not important to prove that the flood happened. Every individual has the freedom to believe that it did … or not. It is a waste of time to search for the ancient ark. The search itself demonstrates a lack of faith. Faith by its very definition is "belief without proof." There will be persons who continue to search for proofs. They are free to do so. But not everyone who wants to be faithful to their Christian heritage needs to base their faith on the "proofs" others claim for themselves. When the next report of the finding of the ark or some other artifact is offered as proof of an historic faith story, we should take it for what it is … an attempt to prove what only can be taken on faith. Trusting in such "proofs" can only serve to weaken faith in the end.

This begs the question, "Are we to accept the lack of proof of the flood as proof that the flood never happened?" And, a corollary question, "Can we be satisfied with the idea that the flood story is an allegory rather than a reality?" Everyone must come to his own conclusion. Remember, flood stories have come from parts of the world other than the ancient Middle East. These stories have sprung up in different ages. It is impossible that they refer to a single catastrophic event. Even though many of these stories have some basic similarities it is not in the details of the story that we find its importance. Instead, it is our common human life experience that makes the story become important. It is crucial to understand that in our collective religious development, Christians, Jews, those of the Islamic faith and others of other religions have much in common.

If we choose to ignore the possibility that our faith has had a progressive formation that parallels the formation of other faiths, then we risk overlooking the validity of other religions. There is danger in doing so. We cannot devalue any other faith position just because our faith understanding has worked for us. How God is revealed is the purview of God. God did not make human beings to be "cookie-cutter" people. Each person is unique. Each person has value in the eyes of God. Each person has the right, and must have the freedom, to find, see, and understand God in a way that reflects their life experience and the relationships they have had.

I am not advocating that the Christian exchange his religion for another religion. I would not do that for the Jew or Muslim, either. I am saying that Jews and Muslims have a valid way to relate to God and the world, just as Christians do. In plain words, it would be stupid for the Christian, the Jew, or the Muslim to repudiate their individual and collective religious experiences and try to relate to God in a way that is foreign to their past.

If we believe that God is Creator of all and that God loves all creation, why should we believe that God would choose to make some peoples "lesser" than others? God doesn't see it that way! If God doesn't differentiate between the faithful of other religions and our own, why should we? Like those of the Jewish faith and others of other faiths, it is comforting to believe that we have been chosen by God as God's faithful people. That belief springs from our human need to feel worthy ... not from any divine truth of exclusivity.

Premise of Chapter Two

Individuals develop a theology based on personal relationships and experience more than on classical theological
understandings.

CHAPTER 2

"The Influence of Earlier Theologians"

The fact that theologians change their opinions as they learn more and experience more sometimes causes mistrust, though it should not: complete truth belongs alone to God.

--Martin E. Marty. Introduction to A Little Exercise for Young Theologians by Helmut Thielicke. 1962. Grand Rapids, MI: Wm. B. Erdmans Publishing Company.

IN THE BOOK referenced above, Thielicke proposed that every person is a "theologian." The freedom to determine a God-image is not reserved only for those with formal training, but is a freedom that exists for everyone. Those who have chosen to answer their call to the ministry have found Thielicke's words to be especially insightful as they worked with parishioners who displayed an unusual array of theological viewpoints. Those parishioners were not constrained by the limits experienced by those with more formal theological training. The person who sits in the pew is not concerned that he aligns his thoughts with the thoughts with any particular theological position or set of theological understandings, as developed by one or more of the great theologians who have helped to forge modern day Christianity. The person in the pew is concerned only with finding answers about God and God's way that seem to make sense to him in his own unique life situation. His experience and relationships have determined his life; and his theological musings seek only to see how God fits into that life.

As people begin to contemplate the existence and nature of God, and the ways God becomes known to them, they need to have some parameters set for their reflections and ruminations. The development of a personal theology is something quite different from the spontaneous thinking encouraged by a "brainstorming" session in a business setting. It is also different from a theology based on classical thought and the understandings of others. There must be limits within which theological suppositions can be developed. A person must be wary of following random or tangent concepts that might lead one astray; and he needs to have the freedom to adapt classical thought to his individual experience and situation.

There are two major concerns with which to deal as they relate to the act of theologizing. First, it is important that one be free to develop his theological understandings on a personal level. The importance of an individual's relationships and experiences cannot be minimized regarding the development of an individual theology. Second, it is important that a strong foundation of Christian thought, relating to the nature and person of God, be the basis of whatever theology is developed.

Many religious professionals take the stand that an idea of a self-developed theology is risky for religion. They do so for a variety of reasons, but the most likely is that when the *status quo* is disturbed, no one can foresee the outcome. There is an inherent risk in allowing the layman to think on his own. Whenever church doctrine or dogma is examined, challenges can arise. Whenever challenges surface, what has been learned may have to be unlearned. The less strong see this as the start of an unraveling of theological understanding that could destroy the church. They may have a point. However, when a weakness or wound is left to fester, the outcome is a loss of vitality. Some positions taken by the Church should at least be excised, if not amputated, so that the body can heal.

Another likely reason for asserting it is the Church's domain to "theologize" is that the common man or woman might develop a theology that is heretical in its content. This has happened over the centuries; but I trust that God is up to any challenge our musings might bring. Is it necessary to protect God from our ideas?

A basic tenet of theology is that the God-image must be consistent in its application. Any God-image must fit all life situations and human experience. God cannot be seen at one time as loving and at another time as vindictive. The danger in having a view of God that is inconsistent is that God becomes fragmented. Our common picture of God limits God, and makes God no more than a "super-sized" human being. It is understandable that we do this, because we want as close a relationship as we can have with God. We want a God who possesses the finest qualities of our own life's heroes, but no human being or amalgam of human attributes can live up to the standards we set for our God.

The theology of the church in its earliest beginnings was singularly suited to the lives of those who had grouped together in faith. It served them well. The "tribal" God was what those early believers needed. A God that incorporated human qualities was unnecessary. A personal God was inconceivable. Life was so filled with unanswerable questions that it required a God-image that established the supernatural qualities of God. Their God was a God of might, magic, and miracles. That God could answer all the unknowable things of life. Rational thought had no place in defining who God was. To be meaningful, the god-image of any period must reflect the experiences and situations of that time and place.

As time marched on, both the god-image and the nature of the church had to be adjusted to compliment the lives of the "faithful." The church has continually struggled to find its place in the world. To remain relevant, it had to change its form, and more importantly, it had to change the god-image it proclaimed. For centuries, the church has fought to retain the mystical God. When questions and challenges arose about this "magic" God, the answer the church traditionally provided has been, "We must take it on faith." Though our musings have advanced our concepts of God, this defense of last resort still exists.

The church, both Catholic and Protestant, can no longer maintain that its historical teachings outweigh, and therefore invalidate, personal understandings of God. That stance cannot perform the same service for the modern-day Christian that it did for those of earlier times. Traditional understandings may contribute to a strong foundation for our god-images, but they cannot be the only means for us to come to faith. The church needs to let go of some of its power, and reflect the freedom-giving nature of Jesus of Nazareth, who allowed his followers the right to struggle with their ideas of who he was and what God was like.

For many, challenging the place of the church in our religious development may seem blasphemous. The opposite is true! It is blasphemous not to challenge our understandings of God and God's servant church. Challenging our understandings of God is not challenging God. The same is true when we challenge the church. Challenging the church is not challenging God.

When the church is unwilling to examine itself, and allow for new insight, it can no longer answer our need to learn more about the nature of God. There are times when organized religion keeps us from getting closer to God, and hinders our relationship with the God-force that has given us life. We have only to look around us to see the fragmented God-images that exist in our world today. This is true within and outside the Christian community. Persons of all faith persuasions need to struggle with their historic God-images. Every person who claims a relationship with God, no matter what his faith community, is called to examine his own historic God-image to see how it relates realistically to his present life.

We stand at a crossroad. Earlier Christians were able to refine and redefine their faith understandings, which allowed their faith to grow and develop in a meaningful way. They could finesse their images to better fit their life-situations. The lives of the early Christians were quite different from those who lived during the dark ages. Those who lived in the dark ages were quite different from those who lived during the Crusades. Those who lived during the Renaissance were different from those who lived at the beginning of the scientific age. We are different from all of them.

During those periods, the god-image changed from one that was magical and mystical to one that met the changing standards of the Church. God's nature became what the Church wanted it to be. As a result, we have been handed a God-image that is unsuited for today's needs.

Those who have attempted to free themselves from the image of God that the Church deemed proper and correct have found little support for their faith struggles. Christians need one another even more than before. Our social interactions and our psychological proclivities take precedence over the dogmas of the Church. Embracing this social-psychological dynamic helps the modern-day Christian recognize and welcome the influence others have on us, and we have on them, and is the first step toward defining a "work-able" theology for our time.

The mystical understandings the early Church had of God and Jesus no longer serve us well in our modern world and the traditional, classical stance of the Church no longer fills our longing for a God to which we can relate. For some, science has "reared its ugly head" to challenge our faith understandings. For others, science has taken over our senses and has become the new religion. The battle between science and traditional religious thought has been waged repeatedly. But this battle is useless, a sham, and serves only to deepen the possibility that traditional religious understandings will be the end of the Church as a viable force in our lives.

Science and religion do not lie at opposite ends of the faith/reality spectrum. They are both God-given tools that can bring us closer to the answers we seek. Questions like "Who am I?" "What is God like?" "Is God glorified by my words and deeds?" and "How do I fit into the scheme of things?" are theological questions that go the heart and soul of our lives and being. Those issues fall under the purview of the church.

"Does God condemn homosexuality?" "Am I unfaithful, if I use contraception?" "Why do we treat women and those of another color and those of other faiths as if they were lesser beings?" are questions of morality. Though moral and ethical questions need to be considered by the church, they are not the main issues with which the church is called to deal. These issues can be dealt with properly by using our god-image and relating that image to the way we live our lives, but often they are dealt with on a moral level, rather than a theological level.

Science can shed light on some moral and ethical issues, too; but science is not able to provide the ultimate answer to all the questions modern-day Christians have. Both the church and the scientific community can help us understand our world. Neither can adequately provide meaningful and complete answers without utilizing the contributions the other can make. Both science and religion fall into a trap. Instead of doing what they individually do well, as they deal with moral and ethical questions, they move out of their special realm of expertise. When they do so, they lose their impact.

Historical understandings of life and the forces that human-kind faced were very different from our understandings today. Without benefit of science, the unexplainable was explained in ways that were fraught with musings that defied logic. The Church relied on feelings of guilt and fear to motivate its followers to lead better lives. The message seemed to be that if we lived a "morally pure" life, we were guaranteed a place in heaven. The Church maintained that what was required of us was to live right, according to its standards, or we couldn't reap God's eternal reward.

But when we deal with behavioral questions, we allow ourselves to become distracted from the real questions of life. "How should I dress?" "Why not smoke or drink?" "Why give to charity?" These questions belong to sociologists and ethicists ... not to our churches. The questions that lead to real life are left unanswered, when we get diverted with lesser issues. It is only when we deal with our relationship with God and our experiences with others that the core questions of life can be answered. As we begin to find answers to those core issues, lesser important questions will be answered, too.

A parent is responsible for teaching us the way through the jungle we call life. The Church is not a parent. It has a different function. Its job is to open the door to life. What we do when we step through this door is up to the individual.

For all too long our religious institutions have concentrated on only one of God's two great gifts to us ... the gift of salvation through God's good will. [NOTE: The theological term for "God's good will" is Grace.] In the process, the church has allowed God's second greatest gift to be almost forgotten. This second gift God provides is the gift of a perfect freedom. It is a freedom to say and do whatever we choose. We can love, or we can limit our love. We can even hate. We have unlimited options available to us as we deal with others and life.

The paternalistic attitude of the Church does little to answer the questions of those seeking guidance. The answers we need go far beyond the phrase, "You must take it on faith." The searching Christian is an adult, and should not be treated as a child who asks "why" without really wanting to know. It is a universal experience to witness a child asking her parent "why" this or that. When a simple answer is provided, another "why" is mouthed, then another and another. That's the way a child and parent interact. Finally, the "whys" have gone on too long and the parent answers, "Because I said so." "You must take it on faith" is just another way to say, "Because I said so." That is not an acceptable answer for the church to give.

This kind of parent/child relationship is evident to some extent in nearly every congregation. It exists in congregations that value tradition and all the drama that sets the clergy apart from the laity in their worship experience. It exists also in the most fundamental and highly conservative congregations, where the clergy may spring from the midst of the people and serve on a part-time basis. The high priest speaks for the Church, giving edicts for behavior. The evangelist speaks for God, instilling fear in those who might stray from the path. Both treat the parishioner as if he were a child.

It is not as obvious, but still true, that most other ministers and congregations have a similar relationship. A part of being human is to want to find the easiest, most expedient way to solve a problem; and the easiest way to solve deep religious issues is to be told what to believe instead of having to work at it. That may sound judgmental, but it is not. Both clergy and laity find it easier to deal with moral or behavioral issues by allowing the leader to tell his or her followers what to do as they strive to survive the demands of living.

If the Church stopped telling its members what to believe about ethical and moral issues and concentrated instead on theological issues, its integrity would be upheld and its impact would be enhanced. Most likely that will not happen. The Church is too deeply indoctrinated with the idea that it needs to be the moral guide for humanity than it is to be the theological standard bearer in the world. As a result, a formula for what constitutes proper belief has been developed and refined. As in days of old, the Church attempts to mold the minds and the faith of its followers. It does little to encourage the believer to utilize the personal resources he has to work out answers for the theological issues with which the modern-day Christian must deal.

An example of this is the ongoing internal "investigation" in the Roman Catholic Church by the "Congregation for the Doctrine of the Faith," the Vatican's watchdog for issues challenging Roman Catholic doctrine. A conservative group of clergy within the Church is attempting to squelch the movement supported by a sizeable number of American nuns to support the ordination of women and to allow married men the opportunity to serve as priests. Several orders of nuns have been singled out as being too liberal and for not concentrating enough on serving the poor and doing work to evangelize the "faith." [NOTE: At the time of this writing, Pope Francis has made statements that may indicate a break with the traditional Church stance concerning the status and role of women in the ministry of the church. The question of married priests is only now being broached on the most limited basis.]

It is not the role of any church to tell anyone what to believe. The most important task of the Church is to deal with its members in a way that encourages them to want to believe in the Divine force it seeks to serve. Its mission is to help God's children learn how to believe, and then equip them in ways to share that belief with others. We need to examine the actions of the Church to determine if it is succeeding or failing in this task.

Everyone has the capacity to deal with the things that are central to their faith. A person doesn't have to rely on the traditional explanations the Church has given over the centuries. One can qualify and quantify what traditionally has been handed him. When he does, a surprising thing happens. Instead of weakening his faith … it is strengthened! No one must justify past theological positions … they can transcend them. The biblical account that has been so crucial to faith development can be engaged in a way that makes more sense for our time. Doing so does not change the importance of the Christian's biblical heritage … it enriches it!

The Christian today has a choice to make. He can blissfully cling to the images of God that have been handed down over the centuries; or he can strive to make his god-image relate more meaningfully to the everyday occurrences of his life. Logically, everyone would choose the latter. If an understanding that makes more sense were available, why would anyone choose to ignore it? There are several reasons. Some simply take the attitude that what was good for those in the past must still be good for us now. Why "upset the apple cart?" Some choose to ignore new thoughts because they are fearful of losing their faith foundation. Others simply follow Church teachings, unaware that it is of prime importance to the Church hierarchy to maintain the present status of the Church.

The Christian church is running the risk of becoming less and less relevant in a world that no longer believes in the mysterious and magical God of the heavens. It is up to each individual to make it more relevant once again. There is no need to fear that mission. God is not waiting in the wings, like an actor-villain off-stage, listening for his cue to make an entrance and do harm to the innocent players on stage. Instead, God is more like a member of the audience, anticipating how the play will end, looking forward to the time when good will triumph over evil.

Unless you are part of a "Christian" group that sees God as being vindictive and just waiting for us to make a mistake so divine retribution can be made, you need not fear. The God I know is a forgiving God. The God I know is a loving God. The God I know offers life, not death. This God is great enough to continue to love us and forgive us and lead us to new life even when we make mistakes while we seek to learn more of what the divine-force is really like. This God is great enough to continue to love us and forgive us and lead us to new life even when we make mistakes while we seek to learn more of what the Church should be. This God is great enough to continue to love us and forgive us and lead us to new life no matter what we do!

We have grown up to believe that God loves not just the good person, but the sinner as well. Our good intentions of trying to understand ourselves and God and our relationship to others and the world cannot be considered a terrible sin. So, accept the challenge this book may bring.

My hope is that you will find things here that will make you think about your faith. In doing so, you may change some of your valued beliefs. Change comes in two ways. First, it comes when we revise what we have formerly believed. Second, it comes when we become more firmly rooted in what we have already believed. The purpose of this book is not to convince you that my beliefs should become your beliefs. All that is necessary is that you think about what you believe. Those beliefs must make sense when dealing with your experiences and relationships.

When we theologize we are apt to come up with a variety of ideas that may not fit together well. It is like putting a picture puzzle together. All the parts must fit. The edges must be smooth. No part can be left out. Each theological concept you hold must fit with all the other parts of your theology. When the picture is complete, your understanding of God and your place in the world will become clearer. God gives you permission to work on the divine puzzle. That's all you need to know to give yourself permission to investigate and challenge your faith. Just starting this process makes you better than before.

The hallmark of any theologian is the proclivity to fight for the theological understandings he has developed. If these understandings are to have impact on others, theologians must defend the concepts they have opined. They "own" their individual theological understandings of God and matters of the Church; and they must safeguard those understandings. Therefore, each theologian must believe that his own concepts are the best understandings of God and matters of religion.

Every theologian must build on the understandings of other theologians; or he must offer contradictory views. It is a main contention of this book that the development of a personal theology is dependent mainly on the relationships and experiences one has in life. These two forces determine the nature of the theological understandings of any person. Theologians, and the rest of us, must have a foundation for their thoughts based on the theological concepts developed by others. Accepting, modifying or rejecting these concepts helps everyone come to his personal theological outlook. Just as any religion develops on the individual and collective experiences of others, so do theological understandings develop. A part of the human condition is to be subject to the influence of others. Both the Church and individual believers are products of the collective force theologians have had through the ages.

An appendix to this chapter follows and details those Christian theologians who have had the most influence on this author. Some are included because of the influence they had on the development of the church. Others, because of the impact they have had on the development of my personal theology. I hope the brief descriptions of their lives and thoughts will establish a framework for your own explorations.

Chapter Two Appendix

THE FOLLOWING THEOLOGIANS are included for their impact on Christianity or for their personal impact on the author.

We begin with **Saint Ignatius of Antioch (c. 50 – 98 to 117)**, who dealt with practical matters of the Church (e.g., how the church related to Jesus, the role of the Sacraments, and the establishment of a fundamental church hierarchy). [NOTE: As the range of dates for death indicate, there is disagreement as to accuracy. Some believe that his death was much earlier. Many dates for persons of the first few centuries must be considered as estimates. From *The Original Catholic Encyclopedia.* Article entry by John B. O'Connor.] If it weren't for Ignatius' influence, we would not have the foundation upon which modern Christian theology is built. Though his concepts were rudimentary, his ideas were sound, given the short time that had elapsed between the life of Jesus and the struggle early Christians had as they attempted to define their faith.

Saint Peter consecrated **Clement of Rome**, [NOTE: Date of birth unknown. Probably born in Rome. Consecrated as Bishop

c. 96 AD. Date of death, 101 AD.] a.k.a. **Pope Clement I**, as the Second or Third Bishop of Rome. [NOTE: There is disagreement as to how many persons preceded Clement as Bishop of Rome.] Clement, like the Apostle Paul, is best known for his letters to the early churches. The only record of his work that has survived is his letter to the congregation at Corinth. His predecessors concentrated on spiritual guidance and moral interpretation for fledgling Christian congregations. Clement took authority for the whole Church through his epistles, bringing consistency to the way local "congregations" expressed their faith.

Moving from the first century, **Clement of Alexandria (c. 150-211)** stands out as an early scholar and teacher of Christianity. He was influenced by Hellenistic thought and the Orthodox approach to Christianity. He was familiar with Eastern Christianity and was a student of Gnosticism. [NOTE: A general term describing various mystically-oriented groups and their teachings, which were most prominent in the first few centuries of the Common Era.] Though venerated by other Catholic branches and even the Anglican Church, he lost favor with the Roman Catholic Church in 1586 due to concerns about his adherence to doctrine.

In the fifth century, our Christian ancestor, **Augustine (354-430 A.D.)**, was of singular importance. He postulated the concept of Grace as coming through the person of Jesus. He also is credited with the concepts of a "just war" and "original sin." He shaped the theology of the Church by merging Greek philosophical thought with Judeo-Christian religious understandings and scriptures.

[NOTE: Mendelson, Michael. "Saint Augustine," *The Standard Encyclopedia of Philosophy (Winter 2010 Edition)*. Edward N. Zalta (ed).] By this time in history, many of the trappings of the Roman Catholic Church would be recognizable to the modern-day Catholic.

Anselm of Canterbury (c. 1033-1109) was a Benedictine monk who served as the Archbishop of Canterbury. He maintained that reason was indispensable to the understanding of Christian doctrine. He founded the "school" of scholasticism, a philosophy that dominated medieval Europe until about 1500 AD. His philosophy attempted to apply rational thought to spiritual concepts. Anselm held that faith precedes reason, but that reason can expand upon faith. [NOTE: Holister, C. Warren, *Medieval Europe: A Short History*. (John Wiley & Sons: New York, 1982): 302.] Anselm's *Proslogium* was an outline of his "ontological argument," which attempted to define God's essence or nature of being in his argument for the existence of God. It received mixed and heated reviews from the time it was promulgated. [NOTE: *justus.anglican.org*/resources/bio/141.] His tenure as archbishop was marked by conflict with both William II and Henry I, when both sovereigns exiled Anselm.

Thomas Aquinas (c. 1225 – 1274) was an Italian Roman Catholic priest in the Order of Preachers (more commonly known as the Dominican Order), considered by the Church as being a prime force in preparing men for the priesthood. [NOTE: Thomas Aquinas. (2010, February 12). *New World Encyclopedia*.See:http://www.newworldencyclopedia.org/p/index.php?title=Thomas_Aquinas&oldid=946794.] He was venerated by the Church as a

Doctor of the Church in 1879 and was cited by Pope Leo XIII as a "great theologian." [NOTE: Scott P. Richart. About.com Guide. "The Doctors of the Church are great saints known for their defense and explanation of the truths of the Catholic Faith. The original eight Doctors of the Church—four Western (Saint Ambrose, Saint Augustine, Pope Saint Gregory the Great, and Saint Jerome) and four Eastern (Saint Athanasius, Saint Basil the Great, St. Gregory Nazianzen, and St. John Chrysostom)—were named by acclamation, or common acknowledgment; the rest have been named by various popes, starting with the addition of St. Thomas Aquinas to the list by Pope Saint Pius V in 1568..." Apr 7, 2008.] Leo required all Catholic seminaries and universities teach the doctrines of Aquinas, including the doctrine of natural theology, which attempts to establish truths by reason without recourse to revelation. [NOTE: Thomas Aquinas. (2010, February 12). *New World Encyclopedia*. Retrieved June 20, 2012. See: http://www.newworldencyclopedia.org/p/index.php?title=Thomas_Aquinas&oldid=946794."] In 1890 Saint Thomas Aquinas was declared patron of all Catholic educational institutions. The clergy of the Church were directed to take the theological positions of Aquinas as the foundation of their own theological positions. Aquinas had great regard for Aristotle, to whom he referred as "the philosopher."

The sixteenth century gave rise to a great number of influential persons in both the Catholic and Protestant traditions. **Heinrich Bullinger (1504-1575)** was one of the earliest reformers, and influenced others who became better known. Bullinger became close to Albert Zwingli and succeeded him as pastor of the Reformed

Church of Zurich. [NOTE: "Heinrich Bullinger". *Encyclopedia Britannica Online*. Encyclopedia Britannica Inc., 2012 Web. 20 June, 2012.]

Bullinger greatly influenced **John Calvin (1509-1564)**, who argued against the Church and was an apologist, one devoted to the intellectual defense of faith that was being criticized or attacked by others. Calvin was concerned with Catholic Church government and much of its literature. His views became the foundation of the Reformed and Presbyterian Church movements.

Thomas Cranmer (1489-1556) was another theologian who was influenced by Bullinger. Cranmer was a powerful force in the Church of England and led the reform movement against Rome by claiming that the Sovereign of England was head of the Church with the Pope having a secondary role.

Richard Hooker (1554-1600). A leader in the Anglican Church, Hooker argued that besides reason and tradition, tolerance had a role in determining church teachings. This stand diminished the importance of tradition while elevating the importance of individual thought and a more open acceptance of non-orthodox views.

On any list of great English theologians, the name of Richard Hooker would appear at or near the top. His masterpiece is The Laws of Ecclesiastical Polity. Its philosophical base is Aristotelian, with a strong emphasis on natural law eternally planted by God in creation. On this foundation, all positive laws of Church and State are developed from Scriptural revelation, ancient tradition, reason, and experience. [NOTE: John Wesley later expanded this Quadrilateral Concept of Scripture, Tradition, Reason, and Experience as a methodology for theological reflection.]

John Knox (c.1513-1572) was a Scottish reformer who was responsible for revising the <u>Book of Common Prayer</u>. His ideas gave birth to Presbyterianism rather than extending the influence of the Anglican Church.

Martin Luther (1483-1546) is unquestionably the most influential of the Reformers. He fought the practice of granting indulgencies. [NOTE: Merriam-Webster. "(The) remission of part or all of the temporal and especially purgatorial punishment that according to Roman Catholicism is due for sins whose eternal punishment has been remitted and whose guilt has been pardoned (as through the sacrament of reconciliation)."] He maintained that salvation comes as a gift through belief in Jesus Christ and not because of the good works one may offer. He directly challenged the authority of the Pope by postulating the concept of "a priesthood of all believers," which contradicted the idea that a formal priesthood was necessary to mediate our sin with God. He translated the Bible from Latin into common language, offering the possibility of personal interpretation of its content, free from institutional bias. On a personal level, his marriage to Katharina von Bora provided a model for protestant clergy to marry.

Huldrych Zwingli (1484-1531) was instrumental in the establishment of what are now known as the Reformed Churches. He, like Luther, openly attacked many of the practices of the Roman Catholic Church. He fought the idea that fasting during Lent was a necessary sacrificial act. He promoted the right of protestant clergy to marry. He established a new Communion liturgy. These three things alone challenged the way the Church dealt with the common believer, held control over its clergy, and expressed itself through worship.

Two prominent theologians of the eighteenth century were **John (1703-1791) and Charles (1707-1788) Wesley**, instrumental in the Methodist movement. Because of their work the practice of religion no longer was confined to a church building. Charles spread his theology through his hymns. He wrote over nine-hundred. John became popular because of his ability to meet common persons where they lived by preaching in the streets, in parks, at work places, and wherever else he could gather a crowd. Both John and Charles were loyal to the Anglican Church, and neither intended to form a new religious group. As their influence grew, Methodist "societies" separated from the Anglican Church where the Wesley family had its roots. John brought an Armenian influence to Methodism, giving the movement a much less formal way of expressing religion.

The nineteenth century gave us several important theologians. From this point on they will be identified by name only. These greats include: **William Booth, Adolf von Harnack, Soren Kierkegaard, Walter Rauschenbusch, and Charles Spurgeon**. Anyone making a list like this might identify different persons as being important. These men and those listed for the twentieth and twenty-first centuries are the most important to the author.

The twentieth century, up to the present, is filled with influential theologians. They include: **Karl Barth, Dietrich Bonhoeffer, Emil Bruner, Frederick Buechner, Rudolph Karl Bultmann, Joseph Fletcher, Hans Kung, Martin E. Marty, Thomas Merton, Reinhold Niebuhr, H. Richard Niebuhr, Henri Owen, Albert Outlier, Letty M. Russell, John Shelby Spong, Helmut Thielicke, Paul Tillich, William Henry Willimon, Karol Wojtyla (Pope John Paul II),** and the present Pope, **Jorge Mario Bergoglio (Pope Francis).**

The relationships a person has with others and the experiences that person has had contribute to the theological position of every individual. The theologians one claims as being significant in his development help to determine an individual's theology, as well. But, even if one is not aware of the influence of any particular theologian, their contact with others who have been influenced has a way of spreading into an individual's theological concepts. Theology operates on "the contagion principle." Theology is passed from one person to another. Everyone who is a part of a person's life experiences has a role in the spread of faith understandings. Therefore, everyone becomes and is a theologian.

Part Two

The Future

Premise of Chapter Three

The Godhead is better understood as a force or action rather than as a person, emphasizing the early Jewish understanding of Yahweh (YHVH), revealing God as "I am" or "I am becoming." In this sense God is more a verb than a noun.

CHAPTER 3

"The Trinity Redefined ... The Godhead"

Then Paul stood in front of the Areopagus and said, "Athenians, I see how extremely religious you are in every way. For as I went through the city and looked carefully at the objects of your worship, I found among them an altar with the inscription, 'To an unknown god.' What therefore you worship as unknown, this I proclaim to you.

The God who made the world and everything in it, he who is Lord of heaven and earth, does not live in shrines made by human hands, nor is he served by human hands, as though he needed anything, since he himself gives to all mortals life and breath and all things.

**From one ancestor, he made all nations to
inhabit the whole earth, and he allotted the
times of their existence and the boundaries
of the places where they would live, so that
they would search for God and perhaps
grope for him and find him—though
indeed he is not far from each one of us.**

**For 'In him we live and move and have our
being'; as even some of your own poets
have said, 'For we too are his offspring.'
Since we are God's offspring, we ought
not to think that the deity is like gold,
or silver, or stone, an image formed by
the art and imagination of mortals.**

Acts 17:22-29

These words from the Apostle Paul have stood the test of time. For centuries, our Christian ancestors have tried to explain what God is like, but still we don't know. Our efforts, though well intentioned, are limited by our capacity to understand. We are limited in our ability to put into thought and word what we think is the truth about the nature of God. Despite this limitation, the nature of our humanity calls us to make our best effort, for if we do not do so, we relinquish control of our right to find how we are related to this God who has created us and calls us to be part of the divine family.

The thoughts and imaginings of others who have "defined" God in the past cannot be the determining factors in our own personal search for God. We have been given a heart and a mind that allows us to make the attempt to know God. We also have been given the desire and the drive to do so. It would be wrong not to submit to this basic drive within us, for it would be a denial of our humanity.

The attempt to know God is why we give credence to the efforts and the conclusions the early church fathers made in their attempts to know and explain God's nature. Therefore, the historical statements of faith and the creeds of the Church provide a basis for our own musings. Though these statements and creeds are limited in their nature, they represent the best compromise the religious leaders of their day could make in trying to define God. Without exception, the historic creeds we recite glibly in today's worship settings are statements that emerged through struggle. Those who penned them fought to have their own personal views of God become the "official" understandings of who God is and what God is like. The very existence of the Church and the direction it would take depended on the work of these early Christians.

Their thoughts have much less relevance today than they did centuries ago. We live in a different world than did those Christian pioneers. Like those early Christians, we are faced with a dilemma when we try to understand the nature of God. If we are to come up with a meaningful understanding of what and who God is, we must emulate those who tried to establish God's nature for their time;

and we must hope that our efforts will be at least as productive as their efforts. When we attempt to make the image we have of God more relevant for our day, others may say we are playing with fire and that our actions are nothing more than an attempt to make God into what we think God should be. That is a fair argument, for every attempt to define God has done exactly that.

The argument to such objections is that everyone in his own right is a theologian and that it is the responsibility of each person to try to understand God based on his own background and experience. We do not live in the past, but these historical statements have in part defined our beliefs. They help to tell us who we are at the very core of our being. The thoughts of the founding fathers of the Church have a real impact on who we are and what we think; but so does the impact of current society. Therefore, we are different from those who have lived before, and, because of this, it is crucial that we redefine God for our own time.

The commanding figure of God, sitting high on "his" throne, robed in white, grand in stature, bearded like a wise man, is a god-concept that has lost any relevance it may ever have had. The patriarch God is irrelevant for our day! It no longer has the meaning it had for earlier Christian believers. That image served only to define a controlling God, one who demanded and expected full adherence to "his" rule. That image gave order to earlier theological musings, and it provided the Church with the right to determine God's nature. The Church took the stand that to question the nature of God was to question the power and control the Church held over mere mortals who struggled with their faith. The image of the patriarch God served that purpose well.

The Renaissance Period, including the time of the Protestant Reformation, was ripe with new ideas about God, the role of the Church, and the relationship God had with the faithful. This period gave rise to challenging new concepts and is rivaled only by the theological advances made in the past few decades. It is now quite common for individuals, as well as religious sub-groups within established organized religions, to advance concepts that extend our understanding of the nature of God. For the most part, these individuals and groups have found that the laity is more open than the clergy to the consideration of ideas that in the past would have been dismissed out-of-hand. Many of these groups have refused to propagate the patriarchal God image, and it has rocked the Church to its core. The unrest the Church has endured during these most recent decades continues today, and it demonstrates the need to continue redefining the god-image.

Society has tagged some of these pioneers with the name "feminist." Their attempt to redefine God in gender neutral or in feminine terms has caused consternation for some in the pew, but more so for those in the Church hierarchy, and rightfully so, because these theological pioneers have given God new dimensions. The "softer" side of God is being uncovered and because of this, seeing God as more loving and forgiving seems natural. But these new dimensions have challenged both the patriarchal image of God and the patriarchal structure of the Church.

Because of their efforts, feminism has taken on an evil connotation for many. The societal disruption caused by those who burned their bras and marched for their human rights was disruptive enough when their efforts centered on demands for equal pay for equal labor, equality in the home, the need to be heard as serious individuals and more recently for working to break the glass ceiling. Many who could support these efforts were confounded, when the movement went even further and the whole concept of God's nature was challenged. The efforts of these Christian pioneers to redefine God's nature have rocked traditional religious understandings. It is one thing to challenge male domination in the workplace and in society in general. It is an entirely different thing to challenge the patriarchal nature of God! We owe a debt to those who took on the religious leaders of the 20th century. They opened the door for others to challenge the God concepts that have come to us through the ages.

The 20th century gave birth to another group of Christians who have made a major contribution to the redefinition of God. They are the ones we have tagged with the name "liberation" theologians. This movement, which has come mainly from within the Roman Catholic tradition in Central and South America, centers its effort on freeing persons from whatever forces that oppress them.

Like feminist theologians, those who are described as liberation theologians have a strong biblical base from which they derive their conclusions. They see the life of Jesus as a prescription for the church that will guide it to free those who are oppressed in our time.

It opens the door to debate economic, political, sexual, and racial issues. Further, it challenges the Church hierarchy as it confronts the way the Church deals with its own issues of oppression. In doing so, the image of God is challenged. It forces the Church and society to look at the way God "condones" or "challenges" the status quo.

Both movements challenge church structure and doctrine. Both movements challenge the nature of God. But liberation theology has even stronger support from the person in the pew.

That support comes from the fact that everyone, no matter what his station in life, feels oppressed in some way. Being human, means we have limitations on our ability to survive. Some of those limits are self-imposed. Other limits come from outside sources and forces. Being human carries with it the feeling of being oppressed in some way. So, it is easier to relate to those who have challenged the forces of oppression than it is to relate to those who see God in gender-neutral terms.

We are conditioned to look at life from either the male or the female point of view. Life seems to make more sense when we wrap up our existence in outlooks and terms that have been made comfortable for us over time. Being forced to look at life as the other gender looks at life makes us uncomfortable, and we tend to rebel. It is no wonder that we feel more challenged by "feminist" theology than by "liberation" theology. But both movements are extremely important to our religious development and core beliefs. To a great extent, these two movements are responsible for the way many modern-day theologians question the god-image that has been handed down from generation to generation.

The Church sees itself as having two purposes. First, it is here to glorify God and bring the world to belief. Second, it is to be the worldly vehicle of divine action. When God's nature is challenged, both these purposes are challenged. The root cause of unrest within the Church hierarchy, relating to the revision of the commonly held concepts of God's nature, is not that God's image is being changed, so much as the Church, itself, is being challenged. When what has provided the comfort and security needed to face life can no longer be relied on, it is no wonder that both the leaders of the Church and those in the pew rebel. This helps to explain the spirituality movement that is gaining strength in our society. Many who come from a traditional faith understanding are rebelling against what they see as the political nature of organized religion. The Church hierarchy has responded by holding even more firmly to their core beliefs, and they have found ways to "prohibit" freer expression and exploration of faith issues.

Faiths other than Christianity give rise to challenging the way we see God, too. Though Christianity, Judaism, and the Islamic faith spring from the same history and tradition, there are some subtle and some not too subtle differences, which can add to our religious understandings. Though each of these three religions claim there is only one God, the way that God is pictured is markedly different. That doesn't mean any one of these groups is right and the other groups are wrong in their concept of God. Because of our human limitations and different experiences, we see God from different vantage points. Given this reality, one might argue that we are dealing with issues of perspective, bias and tradition rather than with what is Truth. But we are not!

Instead of concentrating on why one way of seeing God is right and the other ways are wrong, it is more important that everyone be better able to expand his understanding of what God is really like. If God is omnipotent and exceeds anything we can attribute to that divine force, then why put restrictions on how we imagine that divine force can manifest itself in the universe?

The same argument is true when it comes to the other major religions of the world. Those who don't have a Christian background and tradition also have a part in defining God. Buddhists, those who are Hindu, those who make up the traditional Chinese religions of Taoism and Confucianism and all the indigenous faith groups of the world have something to add, providing a more complete understanding of the existence of the Divine Force.

Even those who claim no religious affiliation and those who claim to be agnostic or atheist contribute to defining God. Those who make no faith claim or even deny the reality of God are of value in helping the Christian come to a more complete understanding of God. The person who denies God because of his or her background and experience brings to the discussion important aspects of the workings of the Divine Force in the world. Put simply, those who believe they have not experienced God active in their lives demonstrate that God allows all of Creation to grow and develop in ways that reflect myriad life situations. Some are overwhelmed with God's presence in their lives. Others are more comfortable, understanding life in terms that hold themselves individually responsible for life's impact.

As Christians, who are we to limit others from the conversation of what the Divine Reality is really like? No matter who, no matter what faith understanding anyone may espouse, no matter what the doubt in a divine being may be, everyone has a place in this world of God's creation. All persons exist and operate in the world with God's approval, so why should Christians limit those whom God does not limit? It is up to each person, no matter what his religious affiliation or lack thereof, to sift through the ideas of others to which he is exposed, and to evaluate the merit of those ideas considering his personal experience and religious understandings.

Our scriptural teachings tell us that we have been created in the image of God. If God is responsible for all of creation, how can those who do not believe as we believe be excluded from the conversation? Every person has a nugget of the truth when it comes to defining God. The force of creation includes all possibilities. When we concede this, we draw from a much greater wealth of understanding of God's nature. In the process, we come closer to God.

The time has come to expand our god-image from that which has the characteristics of a "super" human--all knowing, all loving and forgiving, all-powerful and an always present God--to an image that is free from human characteristics. Merely adding the word "all" to whatever characteristic we wish to append to God is still putting a limit on who and what God is like. To be "all loving" doesn't do justice to God's kind of love. It still limits God by our ideas of what love is like. The limiting nature of human love, no matter how grand that love may be, is still a love that has at its center self-love. We imagine what total love and acceptance of others might be like. What we imagine can't begin to fulfill the reality of God's love, because our imaginings are restricted to what it means to love considering what that love provides us in our own existence. For example, a parent is conflicted when dealing with his child in a loving way. The parent wants the child to be able to experience the freedom to experiment with the options life holds for the child. The parent hopes the child will take a path that leads to happiness and success, but knows that it may not turn out that way. Still, the parent offers the freedom the child needs to test out the possibilities of life. At the same time, the parent fears that if the child makes poor choices the outcome will turn out badly for the child <u>and</u> reflect poorly on the parent himself. When this happens, the limits of love come to the fore because of the self-interest of the parent. Feelings of disappointment or fear or shame can spring up in the subconscious of the parent, along with the more desirable feelings of hope and pride. What was meant to be an all-accepting love is degraded by human emotion. God's "all-loving" nature goes far beyond what we as humans can imagine.

The same is true when we consider God's forgiving nature. To be forgiving, as we want God to be, is a desire that exceeds our capacity to know forgiveness without bounds. We mouth the words "let's forgive and forget," but neither act is possible from the human point of view. It sounds good to say we forgive and forget, but how is that accomplished?

The forgiveness part of the equation has strings attached to it. We can forgive only to the extent that our own self-interests allow us to do so. Being human, we are limited to just how much we can rationalize the words and actions of others. To be human means we are limited in our ability to excuse what the other person has done to injure us. Try as we might, it is difficult to deal with the hurt others inflict.

The forgetting part of the equation is as difficult. In fact, it is impossible. No matter how much we would like to forget the hurt others can inflict, once words and actions are experienced, they are permanently a part of what and who we are. We are the sum of our hopes and the hopes of others, and we are also the sum of all the experiences we have had. To try to deny this is an exercise in futility. Perhaps, it would be better to adopt the attitude that we should forgive and forego. In this sense, to forego means we are to "let go" of the situation and not allow it to define the relationship that has been damaged. To truly forget the hurt we experience because of another person's words or actions is impossible. To "let go" of our hurt can be done.

The super-human characterization of a god who is all-powerful has its limits, too. The super-hero god we have formulated in our minds possesses even more strength and might than we attribute to super heroes in comics or on the movie screen. X-ray vision is nothing when compared to God's all-seeing nature. Zapping evil from the face of the earth is nothing when compared to God's power to cast us into an eternal hell for our misdeeds. The ability of Aqua Man to exist in a foreign environment is nothing compared to God, who established the environment.

Each superhero has its limits. Superman is humbled in the presence of kryptonite. The superheroes, the Avengers, can't go it alone ... they must band together to make sure good will triumph in the end. Wonder Woman stands as a feminist hero whose powers equal the powers of other comic book heroes. She mastered many super forces that, until her appearance, had been more normally attributed to men. Yet, a quick examination shows that each of the popular super heroes has real "down to earth" limitations on their special abilities, thereby creating the plots of their stories.

This means that the super-hero god is reduced to the level of comic book super-heroes as "he" does battle with evil (Satan). There is more to the plot of our life stories than this. God has created humanity with a purpose in mind. Humanity is not just subject to the whims of God as a passive recipient in the march of time. Humanity has an active role in furthering the Creation story. It places a great responsibility on each person, no matter what his or her religious background or lack thereof might be. God has more important things to do and leaves the struggle to us. In this sense, the creative force called God enables us to continue our struggles in life with the hope that we will overcome them in positive ways. In doing so, we come closer to meeting our true potential and we end up closer to God.

What about God's omnipresent nature? When we start determining who and what God is like based on our human state, we run into trouble. We take the premise that we are created in the image of God and go from there. Adopting this idea is like constructing a high-rise complex on a faulty foundation. In the end, what we have built begins to crumble. Instead, we need to work from the other direction. We must eliminate the human element from the God equation. Otherwise, God's omnipresence gets creepy. We are left with an image of god, the eavesdropper, always looking for the dirty little secrets we hold in our relationships with others. We create a god who always has "his" ears open and eyes peeled to hear our words and see our actions, so we can be punished for being the humans we were created to be. God is always present, always a part of the life we experience, but this doesn't mean God sometimes chooses to overlook the things we do and at other times chooses to become involved with us. If this were true, God would be just like us, impulsive, and unpredictable.

The all-knowing god-image is an extension of God's omnipresent nature. When we personalize God, and apply human characteristics to this God of our creation, we are left with a hollow God. It is a God who is dragged down to our level rather than being a God that lifts us up to the divine level. God can be omniscient only if we separate the human element from the divine.

If we have any hope of defining what or whom God is like, we must get beyond the concept of "being created in the image of God." God's nature exists in an entirely different realm from our own existence. That means we no longer have the luxury of having a God who is seen as a patriarchal figure or even as a loving parent, as the feminist movement would have us do. This changed viewpoint will be too difficult for some to accept, but, for those who can get beyond our present-day concepts, there is an enormous wealth of understanding waiting to be mined.

We begin the theological transformation by making a change in the way God's nature is explained. Instead of clinging to the concept of the "person" of God, it is more fruitful to define the "power" of God. This frees us to envision a God-Force worthy of our time that exceeds anything we now imagine. There is the certain risk that others may challenge this suggestion as being superstition, and they could rightly do so, because when we deal with an unknown force it conjures up an image of what is done in a séance. But which is better…having a God fraught with the limitations of a super-human image, or, seeking a God who is freed from all the trappings of humanity?

There is value in returning to the state of wonder of the early peoples who knew there was a power greater than them. Those who existed prior to the formal establishment of religion are a part of our religious heritage, just as the early Church fathers are a part of our religious heritage. Remember Abougli, who didn't have any clear image of what God was like? There was no personal God in

Abougli's mindset. He just sensed that something more wondrous and magical and mystical existed beyond his imaginings. That something had control of the world in which he existed. Going back to pre-dated history and jumping to the present day gives people of faith a new start in the process of defining God. What can come of this process is an understanding of the God-Force that has new meaning for the modern person.

Remember too, the early Jewish vision of God. God became known to them as Yahweh, One who could only be understood as "I am" or "I am becoming." To them God was not so much a person but, rather, an action, activity or force.

We cannot throw out all the work of the early church thinkers and say their work is irrelevant because they don't seem to apply to our life and times. That would not only be futile, but it would also deny an important part of our experience in coming to faith. It takes away the progress that has been made through the centuries. The understandings and traditions of the Church make up the largest part of our theological musings. The Church has laid the foundation for us to continue examining what God is like. It would be foolish to ignore this gift. It would be foolish also to claim that the issue has been settled for all time. Just as the early Church fathers struggled to answer the questions that are being raised in this book, the faithful of today are called to continue the struggle. It is as important for us to do so as it was for them.

To be afraid to continue the struggle is a sign of faithlessness. Just because there is a new way of thinking about God is no reason to discount the effort. If any faith is to be a living faith, a faith that enables its followers to see better the options for living and for honoring God, it must be a faith that makes room for critical examination of its own core beliefs.

The last century has witnessed a revolution in human thought. Business and commerce have taken the lead in determining what our lives are all about. That is not as true in third and fourth world societies as it is in the more developed nations, but it affects those societies, as well. Commercialism is the god of our time. Even the core idea of God coming to the world in the form of a babe is being challenged. This pivotal event in history for those who are Christian is being minimized. Because of this, the Christian world outlook is undergoing a subtle attack, and it affects one of the foundation pillars of the Christian faith. The birth of the Christ Child is now less important than the modern-day effort to control our own happiness and destiny.

The Christian faith story is being eroded. First, God chose to be revealed in the form of the Christ Child. This revelation challenged the thought of Jesus' day in that God's appearance manifested itself in the powerlessness of a baby born in the humble surroundings of a stable. This revelation stood in opposition to the idea that the salvation of the world would come through the Messiah, a mighty warrior.

The next challenge came after early Christians made the giant leap of faith to accept this new revelation of God manifest in the world. Later religious leaders began to define how this God-revelation could fit into their religious thinking. The statements of faith and creeds of the early church attempted to make clear God's nature, and for the most part their influence has been accepted as being the ground of the Christian faith; but it is no longer as compelling as it was. The change in theological thought and religious practice is taking place at an ever-increasing rate.

Beginning in the twentieth century and continuing to the present day, societal influences have taken the reins of driving our religious concepts. We have moved from the idea of God being revealed in the person of an innocent infant, without the means of protecting himself, to seeing God as being revealed in the lives of "saintly" persons. For a while both understandings stood side by side. But now, the infant child's theological influence is giving way to the idea that God is revealed in the lives and deeds of the "good" persons of the world. The list of those persons seems endless and is being added to even now. The Church makes a concerted effort to identify and "test" the lives of these persons to add them to the list of saintly guides.

On this list of Saints was one by the name of Nicholas of Myra, the patron Saint of several groups of society, including being the patron Saint of children. His influence was so great that he became the patron Saint of the Byzantine Catholic Church. He was known for his great generosity and for secret gift giving during his life. After his death, he was venerated for the many miracles that occurred through the intercession of his name. Over time, the Christmas story has been intertwined with Nicholas's life and he has become the Church's symbol of a saintly Wise Man.

The Christian of today is witness to another major change in understanding the point of the Christmas story. Saint Nicholas has become Saint Nick, who has become Santa, the giver of good things to all the good people of the world. Commerce has taken hold of this good concept of giving to others and has twisted its good intent to something that is crass and self-serving. The change is both subtle and, at the same time, blatant.

The Christian's search for the true meaning of life by giving to the innocent, the poor, and the needy has been superseded by the idea of giving to gratify ourselves. The Christ Child's influence has been tempered. The core idea of God coming into the world without might and majesty to bring the world to "him," has gradually become less important. The idea of emulating the saintly lives of others to bring about the Kingdom of God has become more important.

It seems also that the impact of saintly living is giving way to self-interest. The modern-day Christian has relinquished the concept of giving to others to allow them to become better persons. Now, the idea that it is every person for himself is coming to the fore. Taking care of "number one" rests subtly somewhere in the modern mind. Witness the stampeding crowds that are ready to fight one another to be the first to get the limited "Black Friday Special" before neighbors can get it.

Even the Church, itself, has acceded to the power of commercialism. To combat this, pastors have begun to encourage "alternate" gift giving to others. This "alternate" way of giving allows a person to be recognized as being important in the life of the giver, while providing a gift that promotes the wellbeing of some group or other person in the name of the one being recognized. It is an "honor" gift for the one being recognized, and a tangible gift to someone in need. By doing this, pastors help their congregations see that the gifts normally given reflect the commercial interests of society. The caring gifts of alternative giving show the importance of giving to others who may be in more need.

Another phenomenon has surfaced. To be politically correct, the commercial interests of society have convinced us that wishing others a "Happy Holiday" or offering "Season's Greetings" is the way to go to avoid offending those not of the Christian faith. I have no quarrel with that. Not recognizing the importance others place in their own faith expressions is wrong. What disturbs me is the fact that even in the confines of the Christian church building, many have opted not to offer Christmas wishes to others of their own faith group. Societal influences are intruding on even the most basic ways we recognize and honor the importance of our Christian ties to one another.

Don't confuse the identification of this movement as mere whining for what has been lost. Pointing out what has happened goes far beyond pining for the "good old days." The modern-day Christian is witness to a dramatic theological shift in thinking.

Individually and collectively we are responsible for a major change in our faith set of beliefs.

We are who we are because of our traditions and understandings. God is who God is because of our concepts. The idea of a God, whom we have created in our image, reveals the problems associated with that image which now exists in the world.

<u>There is a better way of understanding God!</u>

We develop new understandings of each other and our surroundings when we examine the experiences we have in our daily lives. Some of those examinations come easily and quickly and as a result are not too troublesome. Others require long and detailed work to satisfy our longing for better understandings.

Understanding our surroundings develops as we experience new situations and as we tackle new challenges to our existence. For instance, we gain new insight into the impact humanity has on our environment as we struggle to find ways to deal with the issue of global warming. Some deny the concept of global warming is real or significant or subject to remediation. Others take the issue for granted and struggle to find ways to subdue the consequences they see as dire and inevitable. The lack of consensus is not unusual. It is part of the process that we must go through to understand the world in which we live. This process makes us grow, even though going through the process makes us uncomfortable.

Understanding our relationships develops as we experience new situations in which those relationships are tested. When a child decides that going into the family business is not the thing to do, it causes stress to the parent who never questioned that he would continue the line of family members and become an extension of their lives and work. When this struggle occurs, it is uncomfortable for both the child and the parent. It can have terrible consequences ... or a new bond and level of understanding can come about. Some would argue that the process of going through the struggle is unnecessary; but when it happens, new potential for understanding personal relationships can come about.

Understanding our relationship with God develops in much the same way as the way we understand our family relationships or our relationship to the world. The experiences we have help to determine our outlook on and understanding of everything. Humanity is at a pivotal time in history. Exciting possibilities lie ahead.

Theological understandings have changed from superstition prior to the establishment of organized religion. Theological understandings have been undergoing a change from the patriarchal image developed by the early Church fathers. Theological understandings are being influenced by the understandings of the feminist and liberation theologians of the past few decades.

This change in theological understandings may make us uncomfortable, but it is all part of the creative force of God. The biblical writer of the story of Creation, which appears in the first chapter of Genesis, could have expressed it in these terms.

"Then God said, "Let us give humankind a new understanding of its place in this world I have made. It is necessary that those of my creation know that I am God and that they are my people; that I love them and give them the freedom they need to comprehend my love. My power and my might can withstand their limited attempts to define me and my ways."

"And it was so. God looked around at all the people of the world, and God saw that they were good. And there was evening and there was morning, the seventh day."

No doubt some who look at this attempt to paraphrase the style of the biblical writer will feel that this is blaspheming. They will cite, "For truly I tell you, until heaven and earth pass away, not one letter (iota), not one stroke of a letter, will pass from the law until all is accomplished." Matt.5:18. They will maintain that nothing in the Bible is fair game that would change or expand its literal meaning. They will say that the Bible is the sacred word of God and that those who toy with it are doomed to a lasting hell. If they are right, so be it. If they are wrong, we have the freedom to see God in a new and wondrous light.

So, how does this freedom become reality?

If we choose to understand God in non-traditional terms, and instead see God as a power or force in the universe, we have a new beginning.

The first step is to eliminate the concept of the "person" of God. Doing so seems quite foreign, for at the center of our ideas about God is the idea that we have been created in the image of God. By eliminating the personal God, there is no one with whom to bargain and negotiate, and that is a scary thought. It is harder to relate to a divine-force than it is to a divine "person." We are conditioned to relate to a good "Father," who gives life and who provides direction for living. After all, didn't Jesus, himself, refer to God as "Father"? Everything we have learned about God revolves around this theological concept. It is the part of God that allows us to picture ourselves in the image of God.

That picture of God has some serious drawbacks. How can the person who has had a miserable relationship with her biological father, or who has been orphaned by her father, or who has simply seen all the weaknesses and limitations of a father who has failed in his duty to guide and protect, see the picture of a Divine entity? Seeing God in terms of "Father" brings God down to the human level rather than lifting us up to the divine hope God has for human existence.

Feminist theologians recognized this limitation, and ventured into the dangerous realm of trying to redefine God, using female characteristics. They pointed to biblical images that included gentle characteristics and they freed humanity to be able better to relate to a God who was "loving" and "nurturing" and "forgiving" -- more like a compassionate mother than a dictatorial father, who allowed for no leeway in living a "righteous" life.

Theological pioneers like Letty Russell of the Yale Divinity School were able to couple feminist theology with an ecumenical understanding, enabling the Church to begin reevaluating its understanding of God at work in the Church and in the world. The new understandings gained through Russell's work and others who followed her have opened the door to seeing God in a new light.

Religious understandings and expressions, which began in the realm of superstition, have progressed to a more refined and defined understanding of who and what God is. The comfort level of understanding God as a "person" with whom we can relate is one that is hard to combat. But if we are to define God for our age, we must be willing to make the effort.

We are part of the scientific age. We have become accustomed to looking for answers to life's mysteries based on scientific explanations. We delve into the nature of matter and find that even the most basic component of matter, the atom, is made up of separate parts. In the last fifty years, our understanding of the nature of the atom has expanded. Our understanding has changed from the idea that each stable atom has a nucleus, composed of an equal number of electrons and neutrons (except for hydrogen), to an understanding that even the basic electron and neutron have components.

Look at the work of Fermi Lab in Batavia, Illinois. This lab is a part of the scientific arsenal of super accelerators which are used to speed atomic particles around underground electro-magnetic "tracks" that are miles in circumference. These accelerated particles smash into other particles, causing them to split the atom into its component parts. We have discovered that even protons and neutrons have parts to them. These parts are called quarks and nucleons. We are still exploring these atomic particles to determine the very basics of matter and of life.

Even more mysterious than the proton and the neutron is the electron. These little "energy machines" spin around the nucleus and are responsible for one atom being able to bind with another, thereby creating the elements. It is these "energy machines" that lead us to see God in a new way. But, before going further, I want to examine the larger picture. For now, let us leave the atom and move on to outer space.

The human creation is but a small speck of life on our planet. Scientists are obsessed with finding other forms of life somewhere else in this universe God has created. Space probes venture to Mars and past Jupiter to find proof of life. As we expand our search, the universe itself is expanding. It seems to have no limit, or at least no limit we have been able to determine.

The popular TV show, "The Big Bang Theory," takes its name from a theory of the start of the universe. This theory is just the beginning of our musings about Creation. It is a scientific theory, and has been derided by many in the field of religion. Sometimes the unknown and challenges to preconceived ideas bring fear to our limited human souls. What doesn't fit into our already held opinions causes consternation. A normal human response is to disparage the new and the challenging. But the God-force would have us expand our search further.

An alternative Creation narrative can be found in the scientific search for life and finding answers about our expanding universe. Abougli's clan was able to move beyond its superstitious understanding of a force greater than they possessed. Modern day humanity can move forward from that point, too.

The key to understanding God is not holding onto the patriarchal image the Church has promoted for centuries. Instead, humanity would be served better by seeing God simply as a Creative-force. As the electron gives energy to the atom and all matter, and as the expanding universe may have sprung from the "Big Bang," the never-ending energy of God continues to create new potential within us.

On a breezy day, we can see the effects of the wind as it rushes past the leaves on a tree or as it causes the prairie grass to undulate. It doesn't even have to be particularly windy for one to feel the sway of some of the world's tallest skyscrapers, as the elements of nature exert their forces on the building. We can hear the wind whistle through the steel supports of a suspension bridge or in the vibration of a windowpane of an old and creaky house. We can't see the wind, but we know it is there. We have evidence of the existence of the energy of the wind.

We have evidence of the energy of God, too. That evidence is all around us. It takes form in the extraordinary acts of kindness and heroism that take place in the lives of people around us. God is present whenever someone puts the well-being of another above self-interest. Sometimes the presence of God is obvious because of the impact that presence has had on others. Sometimes the presence of God is so subtle that we hardly notice. But each time God's energy flows through us, we come closer to being the image of what God is like. We reach our human potential when God's energy makes us a reflection of who and what it is like to be a force of love and support and forgiveness.

Being in the image of God does not mean God is like us, having a personality and a human need to communicate. Rather, being in the image of God means that the force of love and self-sacrifice overcomes us and we relate to others as we can imagine God being able to relate. If we limit that loving relationship only to those who are like us, or claim to be one of us, we steal part of God's dynamic life force from being offered to all of God's creation. The same is true for others. Whenever differences overcome the similarities we have in common, God's life force is diminished.

God is not some grand celestial being, sitting high on a heavenly throne, ready to judge or to bless. God is not a superhuman figure, having all the good characteristics we can imagine. God is not one with whom we can communicate on a human level, like we talk to each other. Communication with God comes in the form of dynamic action ... a force that offers love, forgiveness, and acceptance to others.

So, what is God like? God is energy. God is power. God is emotion. God is an undefined force. God is a condition, as in the effects of temperature and humidity. God equals all these intangible attributes.

When we begin to see God in these terms, God takes on new life and is revealed in the lives of each person who takes that power and energy and emotion to advance the lives of everyone who has been blessed by being born. When that happens, it allows us to communicate with God on the divine level rather than on the human level, and that is so much better than what we have known for so long.

As we continue to examine the possibility of defining God in a new way, I suspect the examination we are sharing in this book may cause even more unrest. But we must continue. If we accept the challenge of changing our understanding of the Godhead, it means our understanding of the role of Jesus must change, too. It also has implications for our understanding of the Holy Spirit. So, let us forge on.

Premises of Chapter Four

[1] The Church must explore more fully the humanity of Jesus to define our role in society.

[2] The divine nature of the Christ transpired only when Jesus fulfilled his human potential.

[3] The gift of Salvation connotes a passive relationship with God.

[4] The gift of Grace encourages an active relationship with God, allowing humanity to participate in God's ongoing act of Creation, reflecting Jesus' partnership with God.

Chapter 4

"The Trinity Redefined ... The Christ"

In the beginning was the Word, and the
Word was with God, and the Word was
God. He was in the beginning with God.
All things came into being through him,
and without him not one thing came into
being. What has come into being in him
was life, and the life was the light of all
people. The light shines in the darkness,
and the darkness did not overcome it.

There was a man sent from God, whose
name was John. He came as a witness
to testify to the light, so that all might
believe through him. He himself was not
the light, but he came to testify to the
light. The true light, which enlightens
everyone, was coming into the world.

He was in the world, and the world came
into being through him; yet the world did not
know him. He came to what was his own, and
his own people did not accept him. But to all
who received him, who believed in his name,
he gave power to become children of God,
who were born, not of blood or of the will of
the flesh or of the will of man, but of God.

And the Word became flesh and lived among
us, and we have seen his glory, the glory as
of a father's only son, full of grace and truth.
(John testified to him and cried out, 'This was
he of whom I said, "He who comes after me
ranks ahead of me because he was before
me."') From his fullness we have all received,
grace upon grace. The law indeed was given
through Moses; grace and truth came through
Jesus Christ. No one has ever seen God.
It is God the only Son, who is close to the
Father's heart, who has made him known.

John 1:1-18

WE ENDED THE last chapter on the Godhead by defining God as an
"active force" or a "power," rather than as a "person." We defined
God as energy, emotion, or a condition, as in the effects of temperature and humidity. God equals all these intangible attributes.

When we describe God in these terms, we discover a vast array of new possibilities for seeing how God can affect our lives. When we define God as action, the relationship between God and all of creation changes. God's action comes not as interventions for which we so often hope and pray, but through the way God has set the world in motion and established the laws of nature and natural outcomes. It is then that we begin to understand that God is not going to do for us what we should be doing for ourselves.

We have been conditioned by the Church to think and speak about God as one who is like us, having a personality and responding to "his" creation, much as we would respond if we had control of the universe. But this view of God has one great flaw. We define God in human terms, but understand God in terms that exceed human capabilities. We can't have it both ways. We are forced to give to God features that exceed any qualities or characteristics we might claim for ourselves. God becomes an extension of ourselves, while at the same time God must remain separate from us. It is at this point that faith is tested beyond our ability to believe.

The Church provides an answer for this conundrum. We are told, "You must take this on faith." Is that answer sufficient? Is it fair to avoid any issue, especially important issues, by supplying a non-answer? The Church is here to enlighten our faith, not to excuse the mysteries of faith. So, what are we to do?

We have been forced to see God as one who is like us, but so different that we can never be at one with "him." We need something more. That has been true since the beginnings of Christianity. The early Christians provided an answer for us, and it was "fleshed" out by the early Church fathers. The historical figure of Jesus became the means of God's revelation. The life and activity of Jesus became the portal through which Christians of every age could come to God. The "Second Person" of the Trinity was necessary so that we had a way to relate to God. Until Jesus came on the scene, God was more of a question than an answer.

Christianity sprang from the Hebraic tradition. The biggest task of the early Christian followers was that of distinguishing fledgling Christian beliefs from the beliefs of the Jewish community. Gone was the idea of Salvation achieved through strict adherence to the Law. Instead, Salvation was believed to have come through the sacrifice of Jesus on the Cross.

That statement does not imply that I speak for those of the Jewish faith and that I understand all the intricacies of the Jewish expression of religion. These pages offer only a basic and simple proposition. It is that in the time of Jesus, those of the Jewish faith had been faced with similar issues to what Christians now face, as they struggle to define the structure and meaning of their faith. Those who sprang from the tradition of Moses, the giver of the Law, were faithful as they struggled with the meaning of their beliefs. The God they defined had many unknowable mysteries like the mysteries of God pondered by the Christian today.

The Jew of Jesus' time was like the Christian of today. The impact and influence of society and the personal experiences faced by the Jews left too many unanswered questions for many of them to continue believing in the same way. Part of the reason Christianity took root in the hearts and minds of those who claimed Jesus as the revelation of God was the fact that, until the person of Jesus came on the scene, no acceptable alternative to established Jewish belief seemed viable enough to claim a following. So, what happened?

In our sophisticated scientific age, it may come as a surprise to find that the idea of the atom was first postulated over four hundred years before the birth of Jesus. There were no electron microscopes that could magnify images enough to see large molecules and human cells. Certainly, there were no atomic accelerators that enabled atoms to be split. Finding that the concept of the atom was known and discussed so early in history bursts our bubble of sophistication and shakes our confidence that we are only now on the "cutting edge" of defining the mysteries of life. The attempt to explain those mysteries is not something new to our age. Humanity has always been at work to discover and decipher the mysteries that confound our search for meaning.

According to the Stanford Encyclopedia of Philosophy and confirmed by myriad other research, a Greek philosopher-poet, Parmenides, put forth the idea of the atom around 485 B.C. His ideas and writings have sparked an ongoing philosophical and scientific battle through the ages. His poem has been debated by many, among them Plato and Aristotle, and later Galileo, Rene' Descartes, and in our lifetime, Bertrand Russell.

The range of influence of Parmenides stems from his concept that "nature abhors a vacuum (void)." The idea of the atom's structure, consisting of both matter and space was a concept first attributed to this wise man of long ago. In practical terms, we enjoy the benefits of the vacuum pump, the barometer, the internal combustion engine and hundreds of other inventions that are commonplace in our lives because of this simple postulate that "nature abhors a void."

This postulate is important for our discussion of the religious impact of the person of Jesus, too. Early Christians were confronted with a problem as their faith began to discount the Law as being the means of Salvation. Moses had given a gift to the Hebrew people. It was the gift of order in their lives. The religious Law of Moses was in many ways the equivalent of the Code of Hammurabi, one of the earliest known listings of crimes and punishments that governed the social behavior of the citizens of Mesopotamia.

The Ten Commandments for those of the Jewish faith were the basis of living righteous lives. The Code of Hammurabi provided the basis for a people to live civil lives. The Ten Commandments were supplemented and enhanced by the many rules and laws that governed everyday life. Nothing, not even the simple activities of good hygiene or the way food was to be prepared, was free from the influence of the Law.

All physical activities, spiritual practices, and mental outlooks were governed by following prescribed rules and regulations. Once the religious and moral order for living, given by Moses, was relegated to a lesser important place in the religious life of the Jew, a terrible void was created. What replaced it was more appealing to the non-Jew and it served to fill the void experienced by the Jew by substituting the person of Jesus for the Law.

We are in much the same position as those Jews who found that adherence to the Law no longer satisfied their search for salvation. One of the major benefits of defining God as a Triune Being ... Father, Son, and Holy Spirit or Creator, Redeemer, and Sustainer ... is that the void we feel when identifying the Godhead as a Power or Force, rather than a "person," is filled by our understanding of the Christ ... that part of God who can rightfully be identified as a person to whom we can relate.

The person of Jesus became the means of Salvation for the early Christian. Later, as the Church continued to define and redefine the nature of Jesus, he became the true manifestation of God ... inseparable from the Godhead. The Christ had a two-fold purpose. Jesus was understood as the revelation of God, and he became the means of Salvation, thereby earning the title, the Christ, the newly anointed One, the new Messiah. The Law was still important as a guide for life, but not as important as the relationship that could be had by accepting Jesus as the means of attaining true life.

This transition was impossible for some to make. For those persons, the God Force had already been identified. Those of the Jewish faith already had a meaningful relationship with their Divine Being, as they continued to be a part of the God Force, living out their faith. By following the precepts of their religion, they could better their world. The faithful Jew could still maintain his relationship with God by the way he followed the precepts of their religion.

For others, the person of Jesus became the most obvious means of connecting with God. What was true then is true for the Christian today. Based on individual experiences and collective understandings, the Christian of today finds himself in a similar position to those Jews who were unable to transition from seeing the Law as the way to Salvation. The powers of reason, the individual experiences, and the collective understandings of today's Christian work together to provide a new set of rules and regulations for living a faithful life. It is a logical extension of the message that the Apostles offered in Jesus' day. The "conservative" Christian of today values adherence to the religious rules for living just as those of the Jewish faith did in Jesus' time.

The thrust of this book has been to define the Christian faith in terms of the way social-psychological considerations impact religion. The postulate of Parmenides that "nature abhors a void" is as applicable to religion as it is to natural science, and it explains how Jesus became the way God was to be known in the world of the Christian.

So, who is this man called Jesus? How can Jesus be part human and part divine? What is there about Jesus' nature that defines our faith understandings and human interactions? Finally, why do we need a new emphasis on the nature and importance of Jesus?

Who is this man called Jesus? The answer comes in a variety of ways. It depends on who is telling the story of his time on earth. The scriptures provide different answers. Still, they are the most important sources from which we can gather information. Every analysis and interpretation of these source scriptural documents is of lesser importance than the biblical record itself.

"Jesus, as seen through the eyes of Mark"

The "Introduction" of the Gospel of Mark in the <u>New Revised Standard Version</u> summarizes the background and emphasis of Mark's writing.

Title and Background

"The early church fathers agreed that Mark's Gospel reproduces the Preaching of Peter. Peter's personality can be found on almost every page, and the main characteristic of the Gospel is action."

Author and Date of Writing

"John Mark was the son of Mary (Acts 12.12) and the cousin of Barnabas (Col 4.10). He accompanies Paul and Barnabas on their first missionary journey (Acts 13.5). Paul spoke of him as his companion in Rome and paid high tribute to his service (2 Tim 4.11). It is believed that Mark is the first of the Gospels to be written, possibly when Christians were beginning to suffer persecution under Emperor Nero. It would therefore be dated about A.D. 65."

Theme and Message

"The book of Mark stresses the facts and actions of Jesus rather than his words or sayings. Although it is the shortest of the four Gospels, it is often the most detailed. Jewish customs are carefully explained for Roman readers. One of Mark's purposes was to demonstrate the deity of Christ. He tells the stories of Christ's ministry, especially his miracles. Mark spends one-third of the book telling the events of Christ's last week on earth, ending with his death and resurrection."

Because Mark is the first Evangelist to write about Jesus, he is not constrained by having to refute or support the opinion of others. Missing is the story of Jesus' birth. As far as Mark is concerned, there is no need to have to prove the special nature of Jesus by sharing the mystical account of the Nativity. For Mark, the important facts about Jesus occur in adulthood. Mark may be seen as being theologically superior to Matthew and Luke, who wrote for different audiences. Mark didn't have to prove that Jesus was the Christ by telling a story of the Virgin Birth. In fact, to do so would have cheapened his account. It was not important to Mark to relate Jesus' birth and life to the Old Testament prophecies that foretold the coming of the Messiah. For Mark, the Baptism of Jesus was the signal event that provided Jesus' power to act on behalf of God.

Mark's account of the life and action of Jesus credits him with being the Christ. All through his account are stories of the way Jesus enters the lives of others and changes those lives for the better. Mark has a consistent pattern to telling the story of Jesus' ministry. He begins with Jesus' coming upon someone in pain or having a need. Next, the reader is drawn into the story by identifying first with the person Jesus meets and second by recognizing that Jesus understands the pain of the one he encounters. Then Jesus acts, and the need is met. Finally, in most cases, the person for whom Jesus has given aid is overwhelmed and wants to share the good news of what happened, but Jesus asks that the encounter be kept a secret, and he goes on to the next event. Each of these events emphasized the healing power of Jesus, but that was just half of his ministry.

The other half of his mission was to teach the ways of God. Over and over those closest to Jesus misunderstood what Jesus was all about. It is no wonder that we, too, have difficulty in seeing the real person of Jesus. His followers tried to make Jesus fit into their preconceived notions of who he was and what he was to do. That effort has continued to this day. We want to make Jesus into the cure-all being who will straighten out the difficulties we face in life. We want him to do for us what we should be doing for ourselves. We have difficulty understanding why, if we believe, life still buffets us about as if we were in a lifeboat rising and falling, the victims of a terrible storm. Time and again, Mark tells the events of Jesus' teaching ministry, which was designed to lift us up and enable us to deal with the things that confront us. He pointed out how to live a faithful life.

Matthew and Luke wrote several years after Mark. The Christian faith was spreading through the known world. It was a world composed of many cultures, having different civil, social, and religious backgrounds. It became the task of both Matthew and Luke to share Jesus' story in a way these different cultures could understand and it answered the challenge of some of the Jewish faith that Jesus was not the "Son of God". First, it seemed important to both these Evangelists to show that Jesus had a special beginning ordained by God. That is why both included the narrative of the miraculous Virgin Birth.

Their versions of the Nativity have provided our understandings of God foretelling the coming of Jesus. It includes the part about Joseph willingly accepting Mary's pregnancy as a miracle from God. It includes the idea that Jesus came from humble beginnings, not as would have been expected, as a revelation of God. It includes the stories of the shepherds coming to the manger and the Wise Men following the Star. It explains Jesus' family having to flee to Egypt after his birth to avoid the wrath of Herod. What it doesn't explain are all the inconsistencies and outright differences in their narratives, unless we consider that these stories were written for different audiences, having different faith needs and understandings.

Their versions of the Nativity were designed in such a way as to appeal to their respective audiences in ways that made sense to them. The audiences of both Matthew and Luke were familiar with some of the ideas proffered in the early church. The special nature of Jesus, as evidenced by the virgin birth, answered those who questioned whether Jesus was the Son of God. The concept of miraculous birth was established in Greco-Roman mythology and in the Jewish heritage, as evidenced in the story of Abraham and Sarah (Genesis 17:15-19; 18:9-15; 21:1-7). The concept has been embraced in several cultures around the world. But the validity of Jesus being The Christ does not hinge on the claim of being born of a Virgin, but in the fact that Jesus was "the anointed one," "the Messiah."

"Jesus, as seen through the eyes of Matthew"

The Evangelist, Matthew, took on the task of writing his Gospel narrative to those who came from a Jewish background. The "Introduction" of the Gospel of Matthew in the New Revised Standard Version summarizes the background and emphasis of Matthew's writing.

Title and Background
"The Gospel of Matthew was so named to distinguish it from the other Gospel accounts. There is only one gospel message, but four accounts of it. So, we have here Matthew's version of the "good news" from God. Matthew's name means "gift of the Lord."

Author and Date of Writing
"All four of the canonical Gospels are anonymous, but the early church fathers were unanimous in holding that Matthew was the

author of his Gospel. Also known as Levi, he was a tax collector. The Gospel was most likely written shortly after the destruction of Jerusalem in A.D. 70."

Theme and Message

"Matthew's main purpose is to demonstrate to his Jewish readers that Jesus is their Messiah. He quotes the Old Testament often and uses the phrase "kingdom of heaven" frequently. The whole Gospel is woven around five great discourses" (or, elaborate discussions designed to make a point).

"Jesus, as seen through the eyes of Luke"

The Evangelist, Luke, wrote to those of the Grecian world. The "Introduction" of the Gospel of Luke in the New Revised Standard Version summarizes the background and emphasis of Luke's writing.

Title and Background

"The Gospel of Luke has been called the most beautiful book ever written. Luke's writing shows him to be a highly educated man, one who wrote from a Greek background and viewpoint. He wrote especially with Gentiles in mind, for he explained Jewish customs and traced the genealogy of Jesus back to Adam."

Author and Date of Writing

"Though the author's name does not appear in the book, early church tradition ascribes this Gospel to Luke, "the beloved physician" (Col 4.14). It is a companion volume to the book of Acts, and the language and structure of these books indicate that both were written by the same person.

"Luke was probably a Gentile by birth, well educated in Greek culture, a physician by profession and a companion of Paul at various times. Since Luke probably used Mark as one of his sources (cf. Lk 1.1-4), he likely wrote this book shortly after A.D. 70."

Theme and Message

"Luke tells us in the first four verses that he wrote this Gospel to give Theophilus (likely a government official) the true and complete story of Jesus' life. One of his interests in writing this book was to show that Jesus loved all kinds of people. In the parables especially, he wrote about the poor and oppressed. The theme of joy is felt throughout the book, as Christ's coming brought joy and hope of salvation to a sinful world."

"Jesus, as seen through the eyes of John"

There is yet another Gospel. It is the most erudite; at least it seems so from his prologue, which was cited at the beginning of this chapter. The "Introduction" of the Gospel of John in the New Revised Standard Version summarizes the background and emphasis of John's writing.

Title and Background

"The Gospel of John gets its name from the person who undoubtedly wrote it—the apostle John. His name means "The Lord is gracious." He was greatly influenced by the Old Testament. The prologue, for example, with its account of the origin of light and life, reminds us of the Genesis account of creation."

Author and Date of Writing

"The apostle John is "the disciple whom Jesus loved" (13.23; 19.26; 20.2; 21.7,20,24). He knew Jewish life well and referred often to Jewish customs. John's account has many touches that were based on the recollections of an eyewitness. The date of the writing was probably about A.D. 85 or a little later."

Theme and Message

"The writer states his main goal clearly in 20.31: "so that you may come to believe that Jesus is the Messiah." He may have had Greek readers in mind. Along with this evangelistic purpose, John wanted to make clear to his readers both that Jesus was God and that Jesus had come in the flesh."

John, like Mark, sees no value in recounting the birth narrative. It was not theologically important to him. John relied on his experiences with others who had been affected by Jesus personally to form his theological concepts. These persons had been eyewitnesses to the acts of Jesus or they were persons who had witnessed lives changed because of the influence Jesus had had on them. Experience and reason were the factors that led John to his theological conclusions. These experiences and John's power of reason answered the question of "who is this man called Jesus?"

It seems clear that by the time John wrote his Gospel he had decided the answer to this most basic of questions about Jesus being the Christ. For him, the nature of Jesus was two-fold. First, Jesus was a man, but that did not provide the whole answer. Jesus was a man on a mission. It is the mission of Jesus that completed John's definition of him. He believed the testimony of John the Baptist, who had identified Jesus as the one sent by God to redeem the world.

"Jesus, as we see him"

What about us? Who is Jesus to the Christian of the modern world? We would be served well by simply accepting John's answer rather than by incorporating all the extraneous ideas and explanations about Jesus that have been developed through the ages. Our human nature requires that each person determine for himself who and what Jesus might be like based on our own powers of reason and our own experiences. It may be more comfortable to let the Church fathers provide the answer. It might be less of a struggle simply to accept the word of a trusted minister or priest in an attempt to come up with our own faith position. It may seem logical to accept the majority opinion of others of our faith communities. All these influences have an impact on us, but none can take the place of personally struggling with the question. The problem lies in the fact that once we have come up with an answer, we are prone to letting that answer stand for all time without allowing new insights and experiences reshape and remold our understandings. The challenge for the modern-day Christian is to be brave enough continually to refine our understanding of Jesus to allow that understanding to guide our lives.

How can Jesus be part human and part divine? It is so tempting to use the answer of the Church and say, "We must take it on faith." But doing so cheats the searcher out of the possibility for truly understanding what is essential for a personal faith. It doesn't give enough credit to the person who is searching for God to be able to think for himself. Instead, it is the duty of the Church and the duty of every Christian to ask additional questions of those engaged in the attempt to understand Jesus' role in their lives. For faith to be real, it must be personal. Faith must spring from within the searcher, based on the experiences that searcher has had and based on the reason and understanding that person has already developed. Some outside source cannot provide faith to us. This places an enormous responsibility on the one who is searching for the answers for living a meaningful and faithful life. But there is hope!

Each one of the gospel accounts gives clues to Jesus' nature. Matthew and Luke distinguish Jesus from the rest of humanity by emphasizing his "special" nature through the telling of the Virgin Birth and all that entails, including the visitation of angels, the lowly nature of Jesus' entrance into the world, the later visit of the Magi and the foiled attempt of the powers of the world to end his life even though he was a child. The modern-day Christian must decide where in his personal realm this story fits, based on his individual set of experiences and powers of reason.

Is it better to take these accounts "on faith" based on the thoughts of others; or is it better to struggle on our own, based on our understanding of how the God Force can act in the lives of people in today's world? God gives individual Christians the same freedom to search and decide which answers seem most appropriate for themselves, just as God extends that freedom to those of other faiths to decide how God is best revealed to them in their own life situations.

Mark would have us understand Jesus' divine-human nature without all the trappings of the Nativity story. He omits all reference to the miraculous birth of Jesus, and instead, would have us understand Jesus based solely on his activity in the world. Mark not only omits the birth narrative, but also most of the words of Jesus. He relies on the way Jesus interacted with others and on the miracles he performed. Does Jesus' life and activity provide the answer we need to determine the nature of Jesus? For some, the answer is "yes." For others, that answer seems lacking. The point is that the nature and person of Jesus is defined in different ways for different people. Rather than having these differences be the reason for separating Christians into different groups, the different understandings of Jesus should be the means of coming to a fuller idea of how Jesus can be the portal of our faith for everyone who chooses him as the revelation of God.

John, like Mark, sees the life of Jesus as being more important to the understanding of Jesus' nature than he does the special nature of his birth. The way Jesus called his disciples from out of the world into his ministry and mission was important for John's under-standing of Jesus' nature. The way Jesus traveled not only the roads of his world but also the highway of his life gave John the clues he needed to decide the divine-human nature of Jesus. The parables Jesus told allowed John to determine how Jesus could fit into the life of others. The simple stories of Jesus revealed the nature of the God Force and how that Force could play a role in attaining true life for the searcher. All these things shed light on the nature of Jesus.

Certainly, the role of the other writers of the New Testament should play a part in helping us determine Jesus' nature. Their wit-ness to the Christ gives even more information for us to evaluate. They provide an extended parameter within which to do our faith search. It is important to take these additional resources into ac-count. These writers, along with the Church fathers and historians and theologians of later times, all are helpful to the Christian to de-velop an understanding that guides him on his faith journey. Their importance cannot be minimized, because they help to complete our understandings in a deliberate and sensible way. It is important to take the freedom God provides to come to faith and use it in a way that reflects the "sacredness" of the Christian's endeavor.

What is there about Jesus' nature that defines our faith un-derstandings and human interactions? The Gospel accounts and the writings of the rest of the New Testament tell of the impact of Jesus on the people of Jesus' time and those who lived in the years fol-lowing. It is generally accepted that the books of the New Testament were written and completed during the first century A.D. though specific dates have been debated. Suffice it to say that these accounts reflect the witness of the early Christian community, and they reflect the developing Christian theology of that period. The canon of the New Testament reflects the theology of the Church fathers of the next few centuries. They were influential for several reasons. The most basic reason was the debate in which they were engaged as to which writings were to become a part of their religious heritage.

Long before the canon (the official list of books included in the Bible) was established, popular acceptance had loosely determined the writings that would be included in the New Testament. So, it was not just the important teachers, religious leaders, and theologians who were responsible for the development of the New Testament. The way these writings were accepted and adopted by the common person had an influence, as well. The attitudes, understandings, and questions of the laity had an influence on the thoughts of their leaders. All these influences contributed to the development of the canon, and helped define the concept of the nature and person of Jesus. For good or bad, Jesus has become a "split-personality" of sorts. He is human <u>and</u> he is divine.

What we are discussing here is known in religious circles as Christology. It is the attempt to understand Jesus as he related to the God Force and to the way others saw him as he lived his life in the human arena. The "God in disguise" concept comes to us through the attempt of some of the writers of the New Testament to explain how Jesus could be so special even when confronted with death. It was hard for them to conceive Jesus choosing to do the things that were going to result in death on the Cross. They saw in Jesus a man who was so driven to serve God that nothing could stand in the way. They couldn't imagine being able to do something like that themselves, based on their own limitations and on the lack of any knowledge or other experience of a person like Jesus. It was a concept that they felt had to be explained away, and they did so by giving godlike knowledge to Jesus.

The human nature of Jesus reveals many things. Most basically, Jesus experienced life as we experience life. Even though Jesus' surroundings and life style were very different from what we know, the human nature to question the things that were happening in his life were as present to him as they are to us. If it were not so, then Jesus could not have been truly human. In addition, Jesus had to have the same feelings and emotions we have. Jesus felt wonder and joy, he felt sorrow and pain, and he experienced doubt and uncertainty. If he was truly human, he had no special knowledge as to how his end would come. He was not working from a script, written by God, any more than our lives are scripted. Jesus was not "God in disguise," knowing what was to befall him. He did not know the outcome for his life, until he came nearer to his death. So, any thoughts we have of his nature cannot include the idea that he had powers special only unto himself that exceeded anything God has given us.

The second most basic thing Jesus revealed because he was human was that we have a potential beyond our understanding to relate to God in a way that leads to a "special" life, too. If Jesus was human and lived out his life as he did, we humans have the potential to achieve much more than we think we can achieve. Every rational person who has ever lived has allowed himself to become the victim of self-denial and self-deprecation. It is part of the human condition to see our shortcomings and weaknesses and allow that vision to limit our potential. The human Jesus shows us that we can be more than we are, when we relate to God wholeheartedly and completely. Jesus becomes our standard for living, and reveals our potential for life.

If this is true, how about the wonders he performed? Does that not prove he was different from us? This is not so much a question about Jesus' nature as it is a question about our nature. To become fully human, as Jesus was human, means we have a much greater potential in the eyes of God than we believe we do. On those rare occasions, we exhibit our full potential, we amaze ourselves; and others see in us special qualities and call us heroes for going above and beyond, when we put others ahead of ourselves.

That potential is revealed in the actions of an eight-year-old who decides he won't stand aside when a classmate is diagnosed with cancer, and instead sets out to raise funds to help his friend's family meet their expenses. Doctors who train endlessly and develop new procedures to bring eyesight to those who cannot see reach their human potential, when they practice their art, not just for money but for the joy of giving to those in need. People reach their full human potential when they decide to travel across the world and live with those who are dying because of lack of good water or food by using their talents to improve their conditions and by demonstrating a capacity to love others the world has discarded. When we cite persons who live selflessly, we are describing the potential that lies within everyone to become fully human. Actions like these are described as humane. They are benevolent. They reflect the nature and person of Jesus, the Christ.

Why do we need a new emphasis on the nature and importance of Jesus? The simple answer is our world has changed. The facts of Jesus' life have remained constant because we are witness to Jesus only through the eyes of those who lived so long ago. What makes us human is still the same, because we know we have limitations as to the amount of control we have over our lives. Another constant is that we are just like the early witnesses and followers of Jesus, seeking to make sense of his life and mission. These things cannot be the reason we need a new emphasis on the nature and importance of Jesus. Jesus is the same. We human beings are the same. What made him the Christ is the same. (Remember when we refer to Jesus Christ we are not calling him by a first and last name. Jesus is the name. Christ is his title. That title means he is the long-awaited Messiah, the Son of God, the means of our salvation and the model for reaching our human potential). None of these things require a new interpretation of the nature and importance of Jesus and his life.

It is the world that is different! How do we reconcile the faith-science dynamic and make it useful to understanding the reason for our being? In the last chapter, we discussed the value in defining the God Force as a verb rather than as a noun. That discussion was necessary because of the changed nature of the world in which we live. The scientific nature of our world understanding dictates the necessity of having a more modern understanding of the forces that affect our lives. The same thing is true of our understanding of Jesus' impact on the world in general and on our individual lives in particular. We have the added benefit of understanding our world in a more scientific way. That understanding is something to celebrate rather than fight against. It is unproductive to position ourselves in a way that looks at science as being an enemy of religion. That position serves only to take from us one of the best tools we have for understanding life <u>and</u> our lives. Scientific understandings will continue to have more control of our world outlook … and that is a good thing because it opens the door to improving our lives <u>and</u> our faith.

The Church has taught through the centuries that the main gift of Jesus was his sacrifice for the sins of humankind. The argument persisted that because human beings live in a way that separate us from God, God had to do something to restore us to a fuller way of life. The Church has explained that the reason God came into the world was to redeem the world. In the minds of those of Jesus' time and in the minds of their religious ancestors, that meant God placed the same importance on sacrifice as they did. It was a cornerstone of the way their faith was to be demonstrated. Remember the story (Genesis 22.1-19) of the willingness of Abraham to sacrifice his son, Isaac, as a demonstration of his faithfulness and willingness to please God. The idea of making a sacrifice showed the willingness of a person to please God by offering a gift that could otherwise be used for his own personal benefit.

This story has bothered many faithful Jews and Christians alike. Could it be that it held an entirely different message … or at least one that could rival its usual interpretation? Consider the possibility that the story was not to show the importance of being faithful by making sacrifices to God. Consider, instead, the possibility that it was included to point out that even when we try our hardest to please God, we can do the wrong thing … even be stupid. Perhaps this story was included to show that even the "father" of the Jewish people could fail to understand the call placed on him by God. Rather than using this story as an example of the demand God has to sacrifice to "him," we can use it to picture God in a way that is more consistent with a God who loves and forgives, even when we misinterpret what we should do.

The call God has on our lives is a call to join in the ongoing act of creation, doing those things that will benefit others and make the world better. Looking at the tale of Abraham's willingness to sacrifice Isaac in this way can help to point out our human frailty and the tendency to misinterpret the experiences of life. This interpretation seems likely considering the way Jesus lived. We can see more clearly that God is ready to forgive and accept us. This story shows that God is a force of love. Even little children, who have no theological sophistication, come up with this very sophisticated theological concept about God. Ask them what God is like, and they will say, "God is Love."

It is important to see God as God would be seen. The story of Abraham and Isaac can help do that. The story is more important to us than simply providing an example of faithful sacrifice. Seeing God as one who not only condoned the sacrifice of one's most precious gift, but also demanded it, was to pervert the loving nature of God into something more reflective of human action than of divine action. When this possibility is entertained, it changes the importance of the whole idea of Jesus serving as a sacrifice for the times we turn away from God and God's call on our lives. The understanding of Jesus being the Sacrificial Lamb certainly should not be abandoned. It simply needs to be looked at from a different angle. The whole idea of the sacrifice of Jesus changes the image we have of God through his willing acceptance of death on the Cross.

This has great ramifications for the Church. One of the two Sacraments observed in protestant churches and one of the seven Sacraments of the Roman Catholic Church is based on the concept of Jesus being God's sacrifice on our behalf. The rite of Communion (or The Last Supper or Holy Eucharist) plays a pivotal part in the role of the Church. It is a constant in our understanding of God's forgiveness. The term "Holy Mass" is given to the celebration of God's sacrifice. It defines the meaning of worship. We cannot take that concept away, nor should we try. But we should be open to a broader understanding for why God was revealed in the person of Jesus.

The other Sacrament celebrated in both protestant churches and in the Roman and Orthodox Church is Baptism. For the modern-day Christian, it would be better to raise the importance of Baptism to the level of Communion. Mass in the Catholic tradition is celebrated regularly and often. In the protestant tradition, most churches do not celebrate it as frequently. But in either case, Baptism is not celebrated as often as Communion, so it has a position of less influence, and has many misconceptions. Both protestant and Catholic congregations hold these misconceptions.

The importance of Baptism centers on the concept of God being willing to accept us, even in our imperfect state. Baptism offers hope. It is another sign of God's love. But there is more to this sacrament. While Communion or Mass emphasizes God as being the prime agent in the divine-human relationship, Baptism emphasizes the need for us to be active <u>with</u> God, as we live our lives. The act of Baptism conveys the idea that we don't have to earn God's favor ... it is freely given to all who want to live better lives. It is not an act that guarantees the safety of the person being baptized. It does not hold God to a special commitment that guarantees the baptized a place in heaven. It is an act that symbolizes the need for us to repeat over and over our willingness to work with God in bettering the life of both the individual and the world in general.

God's love and acceptance is free. It doesn't have to be earned. It doesn't come as a reward for good living. God's love and acceptance is something that needs to be celebrated as often as we can. That celebration doesn't have to be reserved only for those occasions when we offer the rite of Baptism to another person who has decided to accept God as the controlling influence for his life. It can and should be emphasized as frequently as we emphasize the meaning of Communion. Because Baptism has a different emphasis from Communion, that emphasis needs to be dealt with on each occasion of worship.

Baptism is an Act of Covenant or Promise. It is a contract between God and the believer. God promises to love us and accept us and care for us. We, in turn, promise to love God, and because we love God, to care for all of God's creation, symbolized by the life and activity of Jesus. Baptism requires something of us. It dignifies us with God's hope that we will be better persons than we already are. It symbolizes the mission God gave us in the story of Creation in the first chapter of Genesis (Gen. 1.28-30). We are responsible for the earth and for each other. We have been given dominion over the earth. We have been created male and female and in the scheme of things the God Force has even turned over the power of procreation to us. Because of these responsibilities, the God Force moves in us and around us. Jesus impacts our lives by providing an example of the way we are to care for others and the world. Jesus is no longer just a vehicle for God's forgiveness through his sacrifice. Jesus becomes the Guide for how to live our lives.

The early church fathers knew this concept well. In their debates over the traditional statements of faith we still recite in worship, they included the description of Jesus as our "Savior and Guide," our "Example and Redeemer." Unfortunately, the Savior and Redeemer part of the equation has been emphasized to the detriment of the Guide and Example part of the equation. Since the time of the adoption of these statements of faith, they have been changed so that what was once an equation is now no longer true.

The hope for the Church relies on making these two aspects of Jesus equivalent again. But, there is a danger of misunderstanding our place in our relationship with God, if we accept more responsibility for our lives and for the world. It opens the possibility for us to see ourselves more in control of things, if we take away the innate power of God and claim that power for ourselves. Perhaps that is why the Church emphasized the importance of Communion over that of Baptism. But, Baptism must be given a greater emphasis because it is the only Sacrament in which we have an active role.

What is the modern day Christian Church to do? By taking seriously the Covenant made in Baptism to see Jesus as our Redeemer <u>and</u> Guide, the Church and we as individual Christians are left with the demand to better our world. We are to deepen our relationships with those with whom we come in contact. Even more than that, we are to foster a more meaningful relationship with those with whom we may never meet. We are to look at the lives and conditions of others seriously and do what we can do to improve those lives. This call to respond to others has a two-fold purpose. First, it serves the world in a tangible way. It helps to free others from the stresses of life. Committing ourselves to the betterment of others makes us agents of God's love for all of humanity. Second, when the needs and hurts of others become our own, we actively participate with God in the mission that Jesus took upon himself.

This is the mission of the Church. All too often the mission arm of the average congregation is given short shrift. We generally value more our own comfort and security. Better furnishings, paying the utilities and higher salaries are emphasized more than giving our resources away. It is the rare congregation that keeps things in perspective. Emphasizing the way a congregation can better the world over the needs of the congregation comes only occasionally and sporadically. The call to action is made, but the level of commitment is lacking. Still, this is the call of God ... the call to love and serve others, as given by the example of Jesus.

It is this two-fold purpose Jesus, Example <u>and</u> Redeemer, revealed through his life and actions, that brings us to discover the nature of the "Third Person" of the Trinity, the Holy Spirit.

Premise of Chapter Five

The nature of the Holy Spirit shows how the essence of God, as the ongoing force of Creation, relates to human existence and individual activity.

CHAPTER 5

"The Trinity Redefined ... The Holy Spirit"

"In the beginning when God created the
heavens and the earth, the earth was a
formless void and darkness covered the
face of the deep, while a wind from God
swept over the face of the waters.

Genesis 1-2

When the day of Pentecost had come, they
were all together in one place. And suddenly
from heaven <u>there came the sound like the
rush of a violent wind,</u> and it filled the entire
house where they were sitting. Divided
tongues, as of fire, appeared among them,
and a tongue rested on each of them. All
of them were filled with the Holy Spirit ...

All were amazed and perplexed, saying to
one another, "What does this mean?"

Acts 2.1-4a,12

In those days Jesus came from Nazareth
of Galilee and was baptized by John in
the Jordan. And just as he was coming
up out of the water, he saw the heavens
torn apart and the Spirit descending
like a dove on him. And <u>a voice came
from heaven, "You are my Son, the
Beloved; with you I am well pleased.</u>"

Mark 1.9-11

... Jesus took with him Peter and James and
John, and led them up a high mountain apart,
by themselves. And he was transfigured
before them, and his clothes became dazzling
white, such as no one on earth could bleach
them. And there appeared to them Elijah with
Moses, who were talking with Jesus. Then
Peter said to Jesus, "Rabbi, it is good for us
to be here; let us make three dwellings, one
for you, one for Moses, and one for Elijah."
He did not know what to say for they were

terrified. <u>Then a cloud overshadowed them,
and from the cloud there came a voice, "This
is my Son the Beloved; listen to him!"</u>

Mark 9.2b-7

Now the Lord said to Abram, "Go from
your country and your kindred and your
father's house to the land that I will show
you. I will make of you a great nation,
and I will bless you and make your name
great, so that you will be a blessing ..."

Genesis 12.1-2

I will take you from the nations, and gather
you from all the countries, and bring you into
your own land. I will sprinkle clean water
upon you, and you shall be clean from all
your uncleannesses, and from all your idols
I will cleanse you. <u>A new heart I will give
you, and a new spirit I will put within you;</u>
and I will remove from your body the heart
of stone and give you a heart of flesh. <u>I
will put my spirit within you,</u> and make you
follow my statutes and be careful to observe
my ordinances. Then you shall live in the

> **land that I gave to your ancestors; and you
> shall be my people, and I will be your God.**

Ezekiel 36.24-28

WHEN DEALING WITH the "persons" of the Trinity, defining the Godhead and the Christ is an easier task than defining the Holy Spirit. The story that follows will ease us into a better understanding of the nature of the Spirit.

The sanctuary was as crowded as one would expect on the Sunday before Christmas. Even those who weren't regular attendees filled the pews. The special music was beautiful, the sanctuary had been tastefully decorated, and the ministers had been especially attuned not only to the historic importance of the season but also to current events and how they related to the Advent of Christ. The atmosphere was electric with anticipation. The time came for the "Children's Moment," and the children were invited forward for their object lesson by the Director of Christian Education. They came forward a bit faster than usual, attired in Christmas finery. One little girl was dressed like Mrs. Claus would have appeared. She had a red velvet dress with white fur-like trim. Other girls sparkled from light reflecting on their sequin-studded outfits. Some of the boys wore ties this morning, proud of being dressed up. Christmas was almost here, and everyone was nearly ready to burst with excitement.

The Director started her talk by pulling out some party hats from the bag she had brought. She had birthday candles in the sack, too. There were other things in the bag to give clues to what the children would be doing when they left the sanctuary for "Children's Church" downstairs. The last thing she had in the bag was a birthday cake. She asked the children why they thought she had all these things. Almost every hand shot up. They blurted out, "It's for a birthday party!" The director asked, "But whose birthday?"

One little girl was close enough to the microphone to be heard clearly: "It's <u>God's</u> birthday!" The other kids and the congregation knew the answer was almost right, but not quite. A few children corrected the girl with the answer, "It's <u>Jesus'</u> birthday!" She knew they were right, and she was embarrassed. She stiffened and answered, "God ... Jesus ... WHATEVER!" The congregation was unable to suppress its glee. The little girl had mouthed something for all of them. It was <u>Whatever's</u> birthday.

God is Father. God is Son. God is Holy Spirit. That is the Holy Trinity. We have an image of God, the Father. It is easy to picture Jesus, as God the Son. But when it comes to the Holy Spirit, many are uncertain. We can't picture that part of the Trinity. The point, here, is that when we talk about God there are many things we don't understand. For most persons, the Holy Spirit is the least understood aspect of God's nature. So, we buy into the ideas of others about the Spirit, whatever those ideas may be.

The last two chapters examined the nature of the first two persons of the Trinity ... the Godhead and the Christ. This chapter deals with the third person ... the Holy Spirit. This third "person" has been known by many names, and has had many different manifestations. This chapter does not redefine the Holy Spirit so much as it recognizes that the Holy Spirit has been redefined throughout the ages, and it continues to be redefined in our time. But the concept of the Spirit ties the other two persons of the Trinity together to help us understand how God is not only real, but also how God is in control, as we use our lives and become a part of the Creative Force in the world.

In some passages, the Bible describes the Spirit as a force "moving over the waters," as in Genesis 1.1-2. It reminds us of the feeling Abougli had in the chapter describing how religions develop. Abougli sensed that there was some mysterious force in the world so much greater than he. In other passages in the Bible, the Spirit has a voice, speaking to a number of characters on behalf of God, as in Mark 9.2b-7. Still other passages describe the Spirit as an influence, personally directing the lives and actions of others, as in Ezekiel 36.24-28. Also, we understand the Spirit to be a part of our own nature. We feel the Spirit as an indwelling power or presence. The Holy Spirit becomes a part of our human nature, and we interpret the best of that nature to be God living through our thoughts, words, and deeds. No wonder the idea of the Spirit is confusing. How do we make sense of the Spirit? Where are we to start?

We begin by separating the three types of biblical manifestations of the Spirit ... the Spirit as a <u>force</u> ... the Spirit as a <u>voice</u> ... the Spirit as an <u>influence</u>. Each of them helps define the

Spirit. Then, we will examine the idea that the Spirit becomes more real as it lives through our own lives.

We find ourselves in much the same position as the early church fathers as they tried to unravel the mysteries of God. An understanding of God as the controlling and creative power in the world was incomplete. Understanding Jesus as the means to relate to God helped, but this added concept still did not sufficiently round out their understanding of God. So, they found a way to make God personally relevant in the lives of their followers. The result was the concept of the Holy Ghost (or Holy Spirit), which became the third person of the Trinity.

The first concept of the Spirit relates to the idea that **the Spirit is a force** that has control of the universe. Deep within the human psyche is the feeling that we lack control over life. Some persons can accept this limitation readily, assuming there is nothing they could or should do to take control from the grand forces that are at work in everything. Others try to wrest control from this unknown force in an attempt to replace God. That need to replace God may be beneath their conscious level, but it is there. These persons regard the universe as their possession, and they can't exist without trying to control the unknown. Most persons fall between these extremes. Sometimes they strive for control; other times they relinquish control. They can't escape the overriding feeling that both their personal universe and the physical universe are controlled by a force outside their influence, and, as a result, they accept the fact that this force has control over everything.

J. Allen Thompson

The nature of the Holy Spirit in many ways manifests itself like the intangible power of a parent. The Holy Spirit can be compared to the activity of a parent of a child going through puberty. The struggle of a parent adapting to their child breaking away from childhood to become an adult serves as an allegory. As the loving parent attempts to prepare the child to become an adult, so the Holy Spirit attempts to prepare the Christian for life. Sometimes the activity of the parent succeeds; other times it doesn't. Sometimes the activity of the Holy Spirit succeeds; other times it doesn't. As part of God's human creation, we can incorporate the wisdom the Spirit offers, or we can fight it, much like a rebellious child might do as he goes out on his own. The Spirit, with all its mystical might, will not do for us what we must do for ourselves as we try to find a place in the world. A part of being human is to know that the Spirit is there and that we can't control it. Its power exists for the taking, but to be fully human, we must be willing to use it for growth and for good. That is how God involves us as part of the divine creative force that has been unleashed in the world. We can use this force. It is freely given; but, if we do not use it, we lose it. By losing it, the Christian fails to achieve his full human potential. It is like finding a rare coin that we choose to drop into a vending machine for a momentary tasty treat, good only for adding calories to an already unhealthy diet, rather than spending the coin for good.

The second concept of the Spirit relates to the idea that **the Spirit has a voice** or a means of direct communication with human beings.

120

This concept is a way of demonstrating that God can and does direct human action. It was also a way the biblical writers conveyed the idea that God revealed the Divine Will to those of "his" creation. Those who have not experienced this phenomenon find it hard to believe or understand these ideas. Belief in this aspect of the Spirit depends mainly on the individual Christian's background, religious practices, and understandings. An individual's life experiences determine the religious understandings of that individual. Every religious belief, including the possibility of God having a voice, is filtered and distilled through the believer's own history.

Theologically, it is wasted effort to debate the reality of this aspect of the Spirit. The Christian (or non-Christian) either believes that God can speak directly to human beings or not. That determination about the Spirit is made solely on the belief set of the individual. Some avoid the question by maintaining that the voice of God (or the Spirit) is an inner voice. Others hold to the belief that God will do anything necessary to communicate with those of "his" creation, and this includes the scriptural examples of this form of communication which are found again and again in both the Old and New Testament accounts, as shown in the examples at the beginning of this chapter.

The idea of God vocalizing directions for living can be likened to the claim of some who have had an after-death experience. Individuals who are convinced they have died have told stories and written books about their experience. They believe that they have been recipients of one of God's miracles so that they could come back and share their experience and live a changed life. It becomes their faith testimony.

Both the idea of God communicating in a voice heard by one of God's choosing and the idea of the reality of an after-death experience are topics that could sideline more important theological considerations. In fact, topics like these move us away from our main task of how to relate faithfully to God. In the over-all scheme of things, they do little to further the understanding of how to be faithful in honoring God and doing God's Will. They conjure up the superstitious concepts and attitudes of the pre-scientific age. God does speak to us, but given the life experiences and understandings of those living in the scientific age, the Christian no longer needs to believe in a divine person having human characteristics like a voice. Suffice it to say that in the lives of some there are experiences that cannot adequately be explained. Even though it might be comforting to do so, it is not necessary to claim a belief in these phenomena to have a strong belief in God.

The third concept of the Spirit relates to the idea that **the Spirit exerts an influence** on all of Creation.

As far as the Church is concerned, it is this concept that is most important. Jesus' earliest followers, like the adherents of other faiths before and after Jesus, had the feeling that the presence of God was a reality in their lives. The leaders of the Christian Church claimed this reality for themselves and for the faithful to the present day. Even some who do not claim Christianity as their expression of faith have the feeling that the presence of God is a reality ... but not everyone does. That is to be expected, given the range of human experience. Not all of humanity will agree with the concept of the reality of God. It is not the duty of the Christian to convince the non-believer that they must believe in God. Certainly, it is not the duty of the Christian to convince non-Christians that they must believe in Jesus. This idea goes against the teachings of the Church since its inception, and on the surface, it violates Jesus' command "to go out into the world and be fishers of men."

At the heart of this discussion is the idea that God chooses the way God will be revealed to all of God's creation. It is not the duty of the Christian to force any particular revelation of God on other persons. Perhaps the most loving thing the Christian can do when confronted with someone who is of another faith, or someone who is agnostic or an atheist, is to give that person the same freedom God has already given them to choose their own faith position. Allowing that freedom can actually be the Spirit working in and through the Christian. When the Spirit exerts its influence, the reality of God becomes more evident than ever before, and our thoughts, words, and actions (or in some cases, our inaction) may be the manifestation of God in the world.

The Christian has too much to do to get his life in order, so that it reflects Jesus, to spend time trying to get someone else's life in order. That is not a selfish idea. When the Christian reflects Jesus through a saintly life, it simply opens the door for others to see the benefits and blessings the Christian has received. It reveals what

God can offer to others in their lives, as well. That is the way the Christian is asked to live … to reflect the love and acceptance of God to all of God's creation.

Now that we have looked at the three main ways the Spirit manifests itself in the world, it is appropriate to deal with the "person" that has been revealed. A part of being human is the quest for understanding the things that surround us and make up our environment. Christians and non-Christians alike should first seek to understand themselves, their reasons for being, and their relationship to others and to God. That complex endeavor determines their identity in the world. That quest continues for some for the entirety of their lives. Others become content to stop the search and settle for the person they have determined themselves to be at some indeterminate time. There are myriad reasons for abandoning the quest and settling for a less than complete self-identity. Sometimes the decision comes from within, but most often it comes from outside forces that convince us we are who we are. When this happens, the spark of life sputters and fades. Not being able to continue the quest, no matter what the reason, limits the human instinct to reach beyond self and continue the search for greater vision and understanding. The concept of living a full life is replaced by the feeling that life is what it is, and because of our human limitations, we have no power to change it. Instead of living, we settle for existing. The natural inclination of an infant to examine and explore is replaced by the acceptance that what is experienced is all there is. As a result, we stop striving for answers. When we do, we abandon the struggle to reach our human potential. The process denies our human value, and it denies the creative force of God.

Some stop their quest simply because those charged with their upbringing have abandoned their own quest. Those in their care have no example or model with which to shape their lives. Others have strong beginnings but the forces of circumstance beat them down, and they lose the strength or will to keep up the search. There are others who settle for half answers; and still others accept comfortable answers, and decide that what they have found is enough to get them through. Many Christians find themselves in this last group. They have found enough answers to make themselves comfortable, so "why rock the boat" and continue the struggle for more?

One of the sticking points for many Christians comes when trying to understand the concept of the Holy Spirit. It is relatively easy to believe in the person of Jesus, a man like us; it is fairly easy to believe in God, a force of creation; but it is nearly impossible to define and believe in the Holy Spirit, the intangible indwelling of God's influence. We have been told through the ages that God is three persons in One. God is "Father, Son, and Holy Spirit." God is "Creator, Redeemer, and Sustainer." Just as the song, "Love and Marriage," goes, "you can't have one without the other," [NOTE: "Love and Marriage," lyrics by Sammy Cahn and music by Jimmy van Heusen, sung by Frank Sinatra in the TV production of "Our Town," on Producer's Showcase, Season 2, Episode 1 (19 Sep. 1955).] so goes the idea of the Trinity "you can't have one without the other(s)."

The Church recognized the difficulty persons have understanding the nature of God. Understanding the divine-human relationship has always been a mystery. In an attempt to clarify the Christian's relationship to God, the Church promulgated the Triune concept of God. This Triune nature helped to explain the mystery and power of God represented in the Godhead. At the same time, the Triune concept provided a means of relating to God represented in Jesus, who, like us, was human. Having a human counterpart to the Godhead became the means of explaining how God was approachable. The humanity of Jesus gave the added benefit of hope to the believer. God was willing to offer a sacrifice on our behalf <u>and</u> at the same time show the potential everyone has in the sight of God. Once the fact was established that God desired a relationship with all who had been created, there needed to be something which allowed that relationship to incorporate the Christian into sharing God's will and God's force of creation.

The Spirit represents that third aspect of God. This triune concept sets Christianity apart and offers the possibility of understanding God in a unique way. The Church provided an approachable God, and it placed upon the believer special responsibilities. The believer was not just to worship and honor God, but also was to participate in God's work in the world. The Christian is not just to be a receiver of God's love and acceptance, but also a giver of God's goodness and grace. That idea is what sets the Christian apart from believers of many other faiths. Other religions command the doing of good, but Christianity sees the good that is done to be an act of the combined goodness represented by the divine-human connection of its believers. To understand God from the Christian viewpoint is to understand that the believer is responsible, along with God, to continue the forces of creation in the world.

The explanation of the Church about the nature of God cannot be the sole determining factor in coming to a conclusion about God's nature. Our human nature requires that each person determine for himself who and what God might be like, based on his own powers of reason and experience. It may be more comfortable to let the church fathers of old provide the answer. It might be less of a struggle simply to accept the word of a trusted minister or priest to come up with a faith position. It may seem logical to accept the majority opinion of others of our faith communities. All these influences have an impact on us, but none of these things can take the place of personally struggling with our own faith questions and coming to our own conclusions.

The concept of God is incomplete without including in that concept the idea that God must be an interactive personal influence in the lives of those who struggle to understand the Divine Force. Removing the human-like personality and characteristics of God and replacing them with the personal influence of the Holy Spirit can best accomplish this. Understanding the divine-human relationship is easier to do when the limitations of a humanized God are removed. It allows the God Force to be dominant in God's relationship to creation.

The Church has defended the concept of a Triune God by maintaining that each person of the Trinity is separate, yet equal, to the other persons of the Trinity. The definition of the Holy Spirit as a divine person equal in substance to the Father and the Son was made at the Council of Constantinople (AD 381). The church fathers wanted to be sure that the believer did not emphasize the nature of one person over another. They wanted to avoid the possibility demonstrated in other belief systems of understanding God as unapproachable because of the might and majesty attributed to their God. They wanted to incorporate a more loving and accepting nature for God, and therefore they emphasized the life approach of Jesus to those he met. The church fathers also wanted to emphasize the responsibility of the believer to God and to his neighbor. To do this, they needed to establish that each aspect of the Triune God, represented by the three separate persons of the Trinity, was equal in nature.

The hope of the early Church has not come to fruition. The Church still maintains its stance, but even before the Reformation within the Church there were some who began to redefine the nature of God in their practice and teaching. For the most part, the Church still emphasizes the same dogma it did before the Reformation. In doing so, it has lost many Christian believers to those who protested both the theology and practice of those in the Church. It was not until Protestant ideas and concepts of God began to take root and grow that the Triune concept of God began to be challenged in the open ... both by theological argument and in practical application. The shift in these beliefs was sometimes very subtle and at other times quite blatant. This challenge has gained strength over time. In our day, the Triune concept of God faces its most serious challenge. The birth of Unitarianism (understanding God as a single person) in the Christian tradition is an example. This challenge comes mainly on a personal and practical level rather than on the level of philosophical theology. It is in the application of theology that change takes root and grows, and how it grows determines the theology itself. The "ivory tower" theologian has less influence in today's world than the individual believer who has been empowered to act on his personal theological understandings.

This is especially true in Northern hemisphere America in the Protestant traditions. It is present to a lesser extent in other places around the globe and in the Roman Catholic tradition. It is evident in a renewed effort of individual faith exploration, and has resulted in two movements.

The first movement has given new life to religious expression through a more contemporary style of worship. In most mainline churches, the member now has the option of emphasizing traditional forms of worship or of using various audio-visual aids and more contemporary music that reflects general society. The worship experience many times reflects contemporary secular gatherings with the congregation offering applause after special music, expressions in dance, or when individual presentations are made. The congregation and even the clergy may be comfortable with food and beverages being consumed during worship.

There is another movement occurring in contemporary society. This movement must be questioned. It should be challenged because it has developed as a hybrid faith expression, springing from an amalgam of sources, allowing the believer to pick and choose the things that are meaningful only to that individual. The movement to which I refer is the "spirituality" movement. Each participant ends up with his own "personalized" faith system that cannot be incorporated into the faith journey of other persons, like most who participate in groups with a more traditional religious expression of faith. The exception to this are groups that demand conformity in their understandings, thereby negating the possibility of an individualized revelation of God. Because of the "pick and choose" aspect on the one extreme and the demand for conformity on the other extreme, spirituality cannot be considered an organized religious movement.

The spirituality movement should be questioned also because it incorporates a variety of religious influences and practices adopted from a wide range of traditional expression, Christian and non-Christian alike. It relies on searching the inner soul to find acceptance and peace. It does not utilize the believer's power of reason enough to answer many of the kinds of questions that religion should be trying to answer. Feelings and emotions tend to replace reason, making it reflective of pre-historic expressions of faith, ignoring the influence of other religions on the continuum of faith development. But the worst aspect of this movement is the emphasis that is placed on providing peace for the individual. Rather than centering on God, the spiritualist centers on self, a misdirection that cannot be overcome. Even so, the argument that those of faiths other than Christianity have the right to express their faith in their own unique ways must be extended to those involved in the spirituality movement and to those who participate in more contemporary expressions of Christian worship.

We are at a crossroads. God has given us the freedom and the wisdom to question and challenge everything. John Wesley, the father of the Methodist movement, was able to identify four pillars upon which his religious societies should build their beliefs. Albert Outler, a twentieth century theologian, defined Wesley's four-fold test of faith, calling it the quadrilateral basis for faith development. There is an acronym for these tests: REST. One's faith should be able to stand up to the tests of Reason, Experience, Scripture and Tradition. The prime factor of the quadrilateral is Scripture, but all four factors determine the way faith develops. In examining questions of faith, one needs to ask the following: Does an individual's belief system seem reasonable and reasoned out? Does that belief system fit into the experiences of that person in his or her life? Does that faith understanding have a scriptural basis upon which to build? Finally, has that belief system had a tradition that has weathered challenges from outside its own tradition? Using Wesley's test opens the door to examine any faith persuasion. By answering these questions, the validity of any faith persuasion can be determined. Though this approach was uniquely Methodist, it carries the call of ecumenicalism to a higher level.

It is common for more conservative and traditional branches of protestant Christianity to hold firm to the "separate but equal" concept of the Trinity. It is less common for those branches of Christianity that fall into a less structured expression of their faith to do so. Given the wide spectrum of Christian religious expression today, we witness a range of ideas about God's nature. The more fundamental groupings of Christianity generally place an emphasis on only one or two aspects of the triune God while relegating the other aspect(s) of God to a much less important place in their understanding. These more fundamental groups generally emphasize either the Jesus manifestation or the manifestation of the Holy Spirit.

Those emphasizing the importance of Jesus over the other persons of the Trinity do so because of the relative ease of relating to God through the nature of another human figure, even though that figure is redefined to take on the aspects of the God-Force. The humanity of Jesus provides the believer with access to God, but then that humanity is redefined, and Jesus becomes less human and more divine. There are several problems with this approach. The most problematic is that Jesus is viewed in a way that relieves the believer of some of the responsibility for being a part of the Divine Force of creation in the world. The responsibility God would have the believer take for himself is refused and returned to the person of Jesus who is then expected to work things out. The phrase "not my will but thine be done" can only serve to cover this refusal to be God's active agent. When this happens, it deprives the believer of the power to be a force for good in the world. But, to the credit of the individuals and groups who take this approach, it puts the relationship between God and the believer into perspective, recognizing God to be in the power position.

Those emphasizing the importance of the Holy Spirit over the other persons of the Trinity present Christianity with a problem, too. In recognizing God as being intimately active in their lives through this mysterious force of the Spirit, they relegate the might and majesty of the Godhead to a lesser status. Though this mysterious force of God can be felt by anyone open to it, it is not the determining power of creation. It is simply the means or manifestation of that power. To view the force of God in life as being the end-all to understanding God does not allow for the creative nature of God. God is more than a force felt in the lives of humanity. God is the creative spark that ignites that force into action.

God is Father, Son, and Holy Spirit. God is Creator, Redeemer, and Sustainer. It takes all three aspects of God for the Christian to understand God's full nature. As we recognize that aspect of God which controls the ongoing creative force in the universe, and as there is a part of God who enables us to relate to and reflect the positive energy of that force, we must acknowledge that there is a mystical and mysterious presence in the world, a "person" of sorts, having a voice and a sensitivity to our human feelings and emotions, an overpowering force within us directing our words and actions on behalf of God. That is not to say every person must see God the same way. God does not have to be understood as having three equal natures. An individual's power of reason and that individual's unique experiences will determine how God will be understood in the end. The image of God that is developed for one person should not and cannot be required to be the image of God for any other person. Trying to make it so violates the freedom everyone has been given to understand God in a way that makes God real. What is necessary is that the theological understanding of any individual must fit together with the other theological puzzle parts of one's faith system in such a way as to provide a clear and complete picture of God and God's way in the world.

Part Three

The Present

Premise of Chapter Six

The use of Prayer and the form it takes define the theological position of the one who prays.

CHAPTER 6

"Prayer"

Rejoice in the Lord always; again I will
say, Rejoice. Let your gentleness be known
to everyone. The Lord is near. Do not
worry about anything, but in everything by
prayer and supplication with thanksgiving
let your requests be made known to God.
And the peace of God, which surpasses
all understanding, will guard your hearts
and your minds in Christ Jesus.

Philippians 4:4-7

IN ITS MOST pure form, theology is the study of the nature and person of God. The word "theology" is derived from the Greek Θεός meaning, "God," and λόγος, -ology meaning, "study of." Plato first used θεολογια (or "theology"), meaning "discourse on God," in his The Republic in the fourth century, B.C. Over time, theology has taken on an expanded meaning, and now generally includes any topic relating to God and the divine influence and interaction on and with humanity. It is a systematic study of the many ideas and concepts of God and their influence on all of creation.

The first two sections of this book have incorporated this expanded understanding of theology. In the first section, the discussion of Aboguli and how his tribe established their religion was a theological discourse using this expanded theological understanding. The same was true for the discussion of the history of the Church and the impact of past theologians. In the second section of the book, the discussion of the need to rethink the divine image we hold, to make it more relevant to the age in which we live, also utilized this expanded theological understanding.

In this third section, it is important to limit our theological reflection directly to the nature and person of God. To do so, we must examine how the concept of sin defines God. We must deal with the role of prayer to see how it influences our perception of God's nature. Our understanding of the forces of good and evil help define God, as well. Our concepts of eternal life help to form our vision of God. Even the rituals we observe in worship have an influence on how we define God's nature. Finally, the way the Bible is interpreted rounds out the way God's image takes root in the heart, mind, and soul of each believer on a personal level. Each of these themes must stand alone for the purpose of this book; but they are interwoven with each other and are dependent upon each other. Without this interconnection, our theological musings become disjointed, and we run the risk of having conflicting ideas about who God is and what God is like.

We are engaged in the process of constructing a picture puzzle, and without all the pieces in their proper place the picture remains distorted. That distorted image can misdirect our thoughts. Our effort is much like what a witness to a crime and a forensic artist do in trying to come up with a sketch of the perpetrator so that the image they develop can help the public identify the criminal. That same process can help to identify God. Remember, a basic premise of this book is that even though we may believe we are created in the image of God, that image is determined by the way we see, understand, and respond to the God-image we personally hold.

In summary, our ideas about prayer, sin, good and evil, eternal life, the religious rituals we practice, and our interpretation of the Bible round out the God-image each person develops. The understandings we hold about these topics exert a personal and practical influence on the way we see God acting in our lives, and they help to determine our relationship with God. A person's theology isn't defined just by a set of intangible and random thoughts or musings. It is defined by explicit understandings of personal and practical acts and experiences. Every religious issue sheds light on the Divine Force. As a result, our discussion moves from the theoretical to the practical. Again, every person is a theologian in his own right. Everyone has a personal concept of who and what God may be, and for most persons that concept develops due to influences other than formal training. Life experiences, the impact of others on the individual, and the random musings of the individual all play a part in the theological development of every person. Let us examine a few of these influences to see how they help to formulate the God-images that have developed.

As we deal with the nature and "person" of God, we first must take the act of prayer into account, for prayer is the most personal of the influences we will be considering. To understand the power and influence prayer has on us, we need to ask several questions. What is the purpose of prayer? Why do we pray? When do we pray? Where do we pray? What do we pray? How do we pray? Is the prayer for God or for us? Does God answer prayer? If so, how do those answers take form? The way we deal with these questions gives clues to an individual's understanding of God.

What is the purpose of prayer? A human being is unique from all other forms of life. Humans are different not just by having evolved physically. We have evolved socially, psychologically, and spiritually, as well. A part of this evolution hinges on the way we communicate with each other. But even more important is the fact that we have devised a way to communicate with God. It is this aspect of humanity that most separates us from all other forms of life. The act of praying defines who we are and what we are all about. The unique ability of the human person to converse with God through prayer sets us apart from the rest of creation. The ability to converse with God provides evidence that, indeed, "we are created in the image of God."

The purpose of prayer is to elevate us to a plain that allows us to feel we have not only the need to communicate with God, but also the right to do so. In the Protestant traditions, no intermediary is needed to approach God. Prayer becomes the means by which we can reason that we are, indeed, special enough to communicate with God without fear of condemnation or reproach. Prayer becomes the vehicle that carries us into God's special realm, lifting us from the humdrum of everyday life and preparing us for eternity. The purpose of prayer goes far beyond the idea that we can talk to God. Our talks are the evidence of a relationship that exists between God and ourselves. Understood in this way, prayer is the most intimate way we can communicate with God. The Church can offer guidance to our prayer life, but it should not take from us the right and responsibility to personally communicate with the Divine Force we call God.

Why do we pray? The simple answer for the Christian is that Jesus taught us to pray, and Jesus, himself, followed his own Jewish tradition of prayer. Prayer for the Christian is a part of our Christian identity just as prayer for Jesus was a part of his Jewish identity. A larger question is why does any person pray?

Each person is unique. Therefore, each person has his unique reason(s) to pray. There is no "one-size fits all" answer to why we pray. For some, it is enough to be able to share with God their joys, their hurts, and their thoughts about life. There is no ulterior reason for them to pray. It is simply an act that recognizes their place in the scheme of things, and it allows them to validate for themselves that they have a place in God's world. It is a subtle expression of their limitations and a verification of God's might. This is prayer in its most pure form, but not everyone prays in a way that demonstrates this understanding and attitude.

Prayer helps to keep things in perspective. A common thread is woven into the life experiences of each person. This thread is the knowledge that no one is self-sufficient enough to be able to deal with all the vicissitudes of life on his own. Every rational person eventually concludes that they cannot tame all the forces that impinge upon him. We see our limitations whenever we are confronted with issues that overwhelm us. It is in these times that we acknowledge the need for help. We go on to ask God to make everything better, as we might ask our parents or our friends or neighbors to help smooth out the rough spots on the personal path we have chosen. Because of this, one person prays for strength and guidance. Another person asks for a sign. Still others mouth specific needs ... get me through the night ... help me with my exam ... let me be cured ... make him or her love me. The list is endless.

Common to all these prayers is the admission that we cannot find the strength from within to deal with all the life situations that confront us. We need help, and we turn to God for that help. In doing so, the nature of prayer changes from its most pure form, which is an acknowledgement of our human limitations and a verification of God's might, to something less pure, an appeal to God to satisfy our needs. Prayers of this nature cheapen the divine-human relationship, for God isn't Santa Claus, handing out gifts to all the good girls and boys.

But what does the atheist do? To whom or to what does the atheist turn? Certainly, an atheist must recognize that he is incapable of overcoming on his own all the life experiences that challenge him. If this is true, how can the atheist survive? One answer might simply be they don't overcome all their life challenges. They exist, they survive, but they fail to reach their full potential. To be fair, the faithful person who recognizes his own personal weaknesses and shortcomings, and who turns to God in prayer, may not be able to reach his full potential, either, even with God's guidance and comfort. So, it is unfair to single out the atheist as being different from the believer on this account. The only difference that exists between the atheist and the believer is that the atheist foregoes the tool of prayer that the believer most relies upon. Instead, the atheist may substitute other tools with which to overcome life's challenges. He may turn to others for help and guidance. He may utilize a different set of rationalizations from the believer to get through life's rough spots. In other words, the atheist still recognizes his inability to survive on his own ... the atheist just uses different survival skills.

So, why do believers pray? They pray in recognition of the fact that they cannot overcome all the problems of life on their own. They pray because they recognize that a power exists which is far greater than any power they individually possess, and they turn to that power for guidance and help. They pray because they are grateful to be able to tap into the energy of the Divine Force that has made them the persons they are. The believer prays because he is thankful for the life he has been given. Believers pray because their prayers help them understand their needs and desires. They pray because their prayers help them see their limitations and their most positive attributes. They pray because their prayers allow them to add to their understandings of who and what God is like. But, most of all, believers pray because they finally admit they cannot overcome all of life's issues on their own; it brings comfort through the recognition that they are connected to God in a way that fosters acceptance of their lives and situation. The act of prayer makes the believer more comfortable. It gives the believer solace.

When and where do we pray? The answers to these questions are determined by several things, some of which come from within and some of which are determined by outside influences. Because each person is unique and has been shaped by his individual experiences and the influence of others, there can be no simple answer.

For some, prayer comes as part of a ritual that acknowledges the mystery and might of God. This aspect of prayer acknowledges the value of community and the importance of others to whom we belong. It is practiced in formal worship settings and in less formal settings that may be determined by the religious groupings of which we are a part. This form of prayer has been practiced for centuries by most organized religions. It may be a requirement of the believer, if that person is to be considered a faithful group member. It is a form of prayer that is practiced by those who find strength in being one of a group of persons who share like, or at least similar, beliefs about their God and the relationship they have with that God.

For others, prayer has nothing to do with worship ritual. It is more an act that springs from the need of persons to acknowledge they are unable wholly to control their own personal worlds and all the life situations that define their worlds. The prayer of these persons at one time may be an act of contrition and at another time an utterance of thankfulness or gratitude. The prayer of these persons may center on the hurts and needs of others, or on the personal needs and desires of the one making the prayer.

These prayers most often forego the ritualistic form of prayer of the group, and they get to the heart of an individual's need in the moment ... a quick prayer that seeks a speedy answer. These prayers are as heartfelt as any prayer can be, but often they are "said" without much hope that they will be answered. They come from a point of desperation, and because of that they define a God who may be understood as being nearly as impotent as the one making the prayer, hoping beyond hope that this God will be able to resolve the issue facing the one who is praying. The good in this kind of prayer is the underlying knowledge that because of our human nature we are not able to resolve everything, as we would like. God is understood as having more potential to accomplish the desires of the one who is praying. The bad in this kind of prayer is the idea that the life being faced by the one who prays may be so tangled that even God is seen as being unable or unwilling to solve the issue. Those who pray this kind of prayer are confronted with the realization that their need not only exceeds their own ability to overcome life's vicissitudes, but their need may even exceed what they envision God as being able or willing to resolve.

"It is the will of God" is one of the most negative ideas that a person can foist on God. It is uttered most often when the will of the believer is out of sync with the outcome of the situation for which a prayer is lifted. When this happens, the believer understands God as being superior to the one who prays, and yet God chooses not to resolve the issue being prayed for in the way the one who prays desires. "If God only knew how much this meant to me, the outcome would be different." "If God only realized how much what was being prayed for could change the world." But, "It is God's will." Underlying that phrase is the idea that "If God only knew, it would be different." God is treated as a "person" or power of last resort. Prayers of this kind subtly limit the concept of what God can do, and this changes the whole image of who or what God may be to the one offering his prayer. "It is God's will" is an admission that we don't understand the ways of God.

The answers to "when do we pray" and "where do we pray" are as varied as the persons making their prayers. Sometimes prayers come as part of a well-patterned religious life style. Other times, prayers are determined by the life forces that impinge on us. The question of "when do we pray" is a sister question to "where do we pray" and the answers to both are interwoven.

We pray whenever and wherever we find ourselves to be. That does not mean that to be faithful a believer must be so involved in the act of praying that it becomes the primary force in his or her life. The committed life of the monk who devotes his being to reflection and prayer is not a life to which most persons are called or suited. Instead, praying wherever we find ourselves to be, means that any place we pray and every place we pray is the right place for prayer to be made. The same is true for the question of when we pray. The times we pray are determined by the immediate needs of the one who is praying. Every life situation has the potential of being the determining factor as to the time and place of prayer. Even if a specific petition is not being made, the need to pray is an end in itself, and therefore it fulfills the need to communicate with God.

Prayer is equally appropriate when made in fear while seeking shelter in a closet, trying to gain safety from the fury of a tornado, as it is appropriate sitting on a hillside, watching a sunrise and listening to the song of birds chirping in the background. A prayer made at the end of a tiring journey is as appropriate as a prayer issued at the side of a child's bed when thoughts of thanksgiving overwhelm a mother or father for the innocent life of their offspring.

What do we pray? The answer to this question is determined mainly by our understanding of God's nature. If an individual views God to be a God who keeps a tally of our thoughts, words, and deeds to categorize that individual as being "good" or "bad" or "worthy" or "unworthy" of love and acceptance, then it is likely that that individual will respond to his image of God in a way that shows deference to the "authority" of the One who knows the "secrets" of that individual's life.

The prayer of that individual will reflect some fear and trepidation as to the way God will react to that individual's need.

It will be designed to mitigate any negative fallout from God in retribution for a life lived out of selfish intentions. In other words, the prayer of that individual will mirror the life of that individual. A person, who because of his life and relationships has a vindictive streak in his nature, will understand God as being vindictive. The prayer being prayed will take this understanding into account, and it will be quite different from a prayer made by one who is willing to forgive himself for his weaknesses and shortcomings. This person's approach to prayer is determined by a view of God that centers on the gifts of grace and forgiveness for the individual. It seems clear that that individual will pray in a way that is nurturing. The individual responds to God based on how he feels God would react to their most private and privileged information.

If an individual perceives the Divine Force called God as being benevolent and forgiving, then the prayer made by that person will reflect the need for a gracious intervention in the life of the one who prays. If he perceives the Divine Force as being judgmental and vindictive, then the prayer will reflect the fear of retribution in the life of the one who prays. This is not to say that the individual is fully aware of this aspect of the nature of prayer. The attitude toward God and the way a prayer is formed may rest in the subconscious mind. Still, an individual may catch a glimpse of this truth as evidenced by the questions often asked in the face of trouble. "What have I done to deserve this?" "Where did I go wrong?" The opposite is also true, as reflected by the question ... "How could I be so fortunate as to have been given this gift?"

148

How do we pray? Let us count the ways. We may speak our prayers so that others may hear or we may do so to clarify for ourselves what it is we really want. This verbal aspect of prayer is best accomplished when our spoken words echo in our ears. It is a way to establish our desires personally and collectively. It is a way of establishing a "dialog" with the only One who is perceived to have control over the random events and movement of life.

We may "think" our prayers so that our wants and needs remain our private possession. Praying in this way maintains the personal connection we have established with God. This form of prayer affirms that we have been given the ultimate place in God's creation, and, because of that, we are privileged to communicate with the One who has control of everything we experience in life.

We may pray to demonstrate actively the desire to be at one with the Divine Force. This type of prayer reflects the concept of a divine-human relationship that makes us partners with God in making the world a better place. If God does will good and love and forgiveness to and for all of creation, then the action prayer becomes one means of bringing about that divine intention. Whenever a person acts to protect and nurture creation, that individual becomes an integral part of the Divine Force in the universe. Whenever a person acts to better the life of another, he becomes a tangible revelation of the way the Divine Force lifts humanity to a higher level. Whenever one acts to mirror what that person sees as God being "alive" in the world, he becomes the means of revealing the Divine Force to those with whom he or she has contact.

How do we pray? We pray in thought, word, and deed.

Is the prayer for God or for us? Prayer is a means of honoring and glorifying God. It opens the petitioner to the knowledge that the God Force can do more for the one who is praying than that person can do for himself. Prayer is a means of humbling oneself and acknowledging God's primacy over all of life. This is true when the prayer does nothing more than to affirm that God is superior to us, even in our best times; and it is true when prayer is nothing more than a petition to God for favors.

Another purpose of prayer is that when a person prays it enables and enlivens that individual to come closer to reaching his full potential. Earlier, the words, "not my will, but thy will, be done," were identified as being negative in their connotation. Those words imply that God is an entity of last resort and might not be as powerful as one would first contend. But here is another reason for uttering those words ... a positive aspect.

Expressing the idea that God's Will is greater than our own, even though we may not understand it, is positive in nature. All too often, when we mouth the words "not my will, but thy will, be done," we subtly limit the image of God as being all-powerful. But, sometimes, we honor God's superiority when we utter those words. Using those words in our most faithful times affirms God's superiority and our human limitations. In those times of faith, the one who prays comes closer to being the image of God we claim to be. Prayer lifts the one who prays to a higher level of existence! In this respect, the act of praying benefits the one who prays. It is an act that is self-affirming, and it allows the one who prays to approach God with the assumption that God will respond in a life-giving way.

There are times in life when it becomes obvious that we cannot make things better for ourselves or for those whom we love. Even in those times a part of our nature is to have hope. Those who don't have hope have had it wrung out of them by outside influences and situations. Therefore, by engaging in the act of prayer the one who prays demonstrates that there is hope even in the face of what seems to be hopeless. Prayer is a demonstration of faith. A miracle is sought. An outcome is hoped for that will triumph over logic. Even in times when the odds of having a miracle granted are minuscule, we cling steadfastly to hope. All this speaks to the grandeur of the human spirit. Perhaps it is in these times that we best become the image of God we so want to be.

The purpose of prayer is not to make our will and desires come true, but to come to the realization that we may not be able to do so. It is fair, and a very human thing, to hope we can make our desires become reality, but if we could will (or pray) things to happen, are we not assuming that our best intentions and efforts somehow can force God to do our bidding?

Let us picture a situation without life and death consequences to help us understand this way of thinking.

Two men are out in the last inning of the seventh game of the World Series. The score is tied. The batter and the pitcher are poised for the final dual for the championship. It is not a life or death situation, but try telling that to the fans. The most powerful batter and the pitcher with the best stats are ready to face each other. The whole season comes down to this moment. Who will win?

In this moment, the ballpark becomes a cathedral. Everyone prays. Is the outcome determined by the effectiveness of one prayer over another? Does the World Series Champion team get to be champion because their fans were better prayers than those who prayed for a win for the other team? Does the batter have a better chance of hitting a winning home run because he prayed and crossed himself as he stepped into the batter's box ... or does the pitcher strike him out because his prayers trumped the batter's prayers?

What are we to think about prayer when two opposing prayers collide and only one prayer seems to be answered? In real life, is the one whose prayer was answered favored by God? Did he or she live a better life than the one whose prayer was denied? Even if we don't consciously view prayer in this way, it puts the onus of the outcome squarely on the shoulders of the one who prays and this is exactly what the faithful petitioner should avoid. When we find ourselves unable to solve the ultimate issues that come before us, our prayers become the means of turning our lack of control over to God. It is a final effort to solve our problems. But that doesn't happen if we understand prayer as a way to bend life to our will. It makes no difference whether we do it consciously or unconsciously. We are not in control! Prayer cannot change that fact.

Is prayer for God or for us? It is for God if prayer enables us to see and recognize our limitations when compared to the Divine Force active in the world. It is for God when we seek to participate with that Divine Force to make the world a better place. It is for God when we come to terms with the fact that life is a gift, even though that gift may come to us with sorrow and pain.

In the same vein, prayer is for us whenever it enables us to see and recognize our limitations. It is for us anytime we find encouragement to actively participate with God in making the world a better place. It is for us as we come to understand that all of life is a gift ... the bad as well as the good.

Does God answer prayer? YES!

How do those answers take form? It may not always seem so, but the Divine Force we call God <u>always</u> answers prayer. An answered prayer is not always revealed in the outcome of any issue for which the prayer may be addressed. The answer to a prayer is not the result obtained. The value of prayer comes from the act of praying. That act allows us to experience the power and presence of God. The Christian, the Jew, the Muslim, the Buddhist, those who practice earth religions and all the rest of humanity who claim a religion have something in common. Everyone can experience the power and presence of a Divine Force through prayer.

The experience of praying reveals the existence of a God who has intricately woven the divine power of Creation into our lives. That is the essence of prayer.

The purpose of this chapter is not to provide the answers to the mystery of prayer and its power. The purpose is simply to ask the questions that may open doors of understanding or point us in new directions, so that we can see the Divine Force of God in a new way. Our separate understandings of prayer help to complete the image of God each person of religion may hold. Even the non-religious person forms an image of God based at least in part on that person's understanding of prayer. How a person chooses to communicate with the Divine Force or how a person sees such an effort to be meaningless adds to the image we have created God to be.

Prayer defines God and is the most personal way God's image takes form for the believer. Prayer is the means of relating personal experience and relationships beyond our individual psyche to the Divine Force, to others, and to the world. Over time, to understand the power prayer holds for the individual, this basic concept of prayer has been lost, and a variety of secondary understandings have developed. In many cases, these understandings have supplanted this basic concept of prayer.

Because a basic quest of the believer is to find a way to be "at one" with God, we are oriented in religion to move from the present toward the eternal. We seek a life full of meaning. To that end, it seems that an eternity with God is far superior to what we experience in the present. Given that truth, we need to make a decision about prayer. When praying, should our main purpose be to serve our self-interest and seek God's intervention for our needs; or, when praying should our main purpose be to come closer to knowing how God can become so much a part of us that we can no longer be separate from God. The answer the believer chooses will determine, at least in part, God's nature and being.

Premise of Chapter Seven

Sin is not any of many possible actions or inaction but is a state of being ... a separation from God.

CHAPTER 7

"Sin"

"Therefore, just as one man's trespass
led to condemnation for all, so one man's
act of righteousness leads to justification
and life for all. For just as by the one
man's disobedience the many were made
sinners, so by the one man's obedience
the many will be made righteous."

--Paul's explanation of how Adam,
(representing humanity) broke the
relationship that existed between him
and God, and how Jesus restored that
relationship for all humankind.--

Romans 5:18-19

THE CONCEPT OF sin is enmeshed with the judgment of what is right
and what is wrong; but theologically speaking, sin has little to do
with our moral evaluations.

The Church is constantly dealing with the issue of sin. After all, the Church is in the business of not only trying to define sin but also trying to help individuals avoid the commission of sin and its ramifications. But, along the way, the Church has fallen into a trap. It has strayed from its purpose of providing a coherent understanding of sin. This has happened for a variety of reasons. The first and most compelling reason is that it has worked backward in its attempt to deal with the issue of sin, itself.

Sin is a state of being. It is not an act of disobedience. So, any attempt to simplify the concept of sin as being a list of wrongs is misleading. It keeps the believer from coming closer to God by misdirecting the believer. In the attempt to simplify things, the Church has built a barrier between the Divine Force we call God and ourselves. By coming up with lists of what is right and wrong, we have turned sin from the original concept of a state of being into the idea that there is a never-ending list of acts that cheapen our humanity. Sin has become a morality issue, but sin goes much deeper than that. If sin were only a question of morals, there would be no hope to overcome it, because we are imperfect, flawed, and subject to temptation.

The Church has changed the concept of sin. It began as a description of humanity's fall from Grace. Sin was identified as the change in the relationship between God and humanity. It has become more of a grocery list of things that contribute to the break in the human-Divine relationship. Because of this, both the Church and individual Christians have strayed from the core idea of sin.

Both the religious and the non-religious have a false idea of what sin entails.

"Church" as used here is generic. The "Church" does not refer to just the Roman Catholic institution. It refers also to other Christian groupings. In fact, the term applies to non-Christian religious groupings, as well. The Muslim, the Jew, the Buddhist, and those of other religions, individually and collectively, have fallen into the same trap. "The Church" refers to any religious institution and even to those individuals who seek to define moral and/or religious law.

<u>Sin is the condition of being separated from God</u>. When the Divine-human relationship is disrupted, sin exists. There are writings earlier than the biblical accounts that have dealt with the concept of sin, but we begin by examining the second and third chapters of Genesis, which is the story of Adam and Eve in the Garden of Eden. The point of the story was not that Adam (or Eve) did something that was wrong, although that is certainly true. These two characters represent every human being who has ever walked the earth. They fell to temptation, and chose to disobey God.

The point of the story is that when someone does something that puts a barrier between God and ourselves, our state of being changes. We are no longer "at one" with God. The difference between our humanity and God's divinity is emphasized, and we come to understand that we cannot be like God. We understand that our human condition and our choices separate us from God. Thank goodness, the story goes on and tells us of God's forgiving nature toward us so that we have the hope of renewing our relationship with God; but that will be dealt with in more detail in a later chapter. For now, it is important to understand that we exist in a state of separation from God but that God still loves those who stray from the full relationship that is held out to us, even though as humans we continually break that relationship. That "brokenness" is sin.

Everyone is a product of his environment and experiences. Though everyone shares a commonality of existence, how that existence is fashioned is unique and special for each person. No two persons are exactly alike. This truth is easy to see in twins who have a common life and are influenced, for the most part, by the same forces. Yet, one twin turns out having a positive attitude about life, and the other is more negative. Their roles in society are quite different. One may be viewed as being successful, a contributor to the good of society, while the other one may be considered a failure and a dreg on humanity. These twins who were afforded the same upbringing and had much the same experiences can be totally different persons.

Now, consider the rest of humanity ... those who have totally different lives and experiences and are influenced by different persons. Everyone is a product of his environment and the relationships he enjoys. The only commonality everyone can claim is that they are unique, different from everyone else. Given this fact, if we look at sin as being an act of disobedience rather than a state of existence, then the "sinful" act as defined by one person will not have the same impact on or be interpreted the same way by another person. The list of sins as defined by any individual is unique to that individual. Each person's list of sins reflects the image the individual has of God.

An exception to this concept occurs when persons accept a group mentality as to what constitutes a sinful act or acts. The individual relinquishes to others his power to evaluate his life situations. When this happens, the collective understanding of "sin" takes precedence over the understanding of the individual.

Examples of this are found everywhere. They are found both within religious groupings and in the secular world. For this discussion, it will be limited to those groups seeking religious understanding. It wasn't too long ago that dancing (and even singing) in some churches was considered so sinful that those who perpetrated such acts were often considered by others, who were more straight-laced, as persons destined to go to hell. Those "proper" persons were convinced that those who broke God's command to be "reverent" were walking the slippery slope of damnation and would dwell eternally in the fires of hell.

Today, fewer persons hold that opinion, as the power and influence of religion has lessened on society in general. Lists of "sins" have no lasting validity and can change as the attitudes and opinions of persons change. It is important to affirm any person or group of people who seek to be closer to God, but a problem arises when anyone seeks to impose his understandings on others, thereby limiting their freedom to relate to God and others in ways that reflect their own unique experiences.

When one person, or a like-minded group of persons, categorizes immoral acts as "sin," they may not always seem sinful to others. So, what is sin? Sin simply cannot be thought of as an immoral act. Instead, sin must be thought of as a break in the Divine-human relationship. Sin must be thought of as the separation that exists between God and ourselves. Sin occurs whenever we cheapen our relationships with others. Sin occurs whenever we destroy the gifts God has created for our benefit and enjoyment. Any time the sense of self overcomes the possibility of a deeper relationship with others, the Divine-human relationship breaks down. That is sin.

To some, sin seems to lose its power if we cannot define it in concrete terms. Sin seems to have no meaning if we cannot identify specific "bad" acts. Lists of sins take on great importance because those lists reflect the broken relationship that occurs when God's creative Will for good is stifled. The creative Force that we call God permeates everything. Each moment of life is a moment that can strengthen that force or interfere with it. When one chooses to join God's force for good, sin is destroyed. When one chooses to fight God's force for good, sin is the result.

There is a classic exercise that helps to picture the nature of sin. In the center of a sheet of paper draw the image of God you have in your mind. It doesn't matter what it looks like. The image must be personal. It can be the classic "Father" figure of a man in a flowing robe with a white beard, holding a staff, sitting on a throne. Or it can be a Mother Hen, sheltering her brood. Or it can be a Whirlwind or a Source of Light or anything else that pictures the Divine Force for you. From that God image draw arrows outward in all directions as light radiates from the sun. Those arrows represent the power and influence of God over all creation. Now, draw a small stick figure anywhere beyond the range of arrows. That stick figure is you. You cannot exist alone, so continue drawing other stick figures on the sheet beyond the arrows in a circle around God. Picture that circle of stick figures all turned toward God. When the figures stand facing God, the force of the arrows speeds toward them with all the power and might and love and compassion God sends our way. We bask in the warmth of God's love as if we were on a beach feeling the sun on our faces. We are in harmony with God, and we feel God's warm concern for us ... and all is good. Now, picture that circle of stick figures all turned away from God toward the edge of the sheet. We can no longer see God and the arrows seem to fly past us out beyond the sheet, and they have no effect on us. Gone is the warmth we felt before. We can no longer see God, and we can't even see the other figures in the circle. It seems we are lost and alone. When we are turned toward God we feel the relationship we have with not only our God but also with the others in our sphere of life. When we are turned away from God the relationship is broken. That is sin.

Life is more complex than our simple drawing shows. The figure of the God-Force in the center remains constant. The piece of paper represents the universe, but the universe is not finite. It continues without end. Both the physical universe and our own personal universe are continually expanding ... they have no end. When considering the question of sin, we are dealing with a continual strain on our relationship with others and with God. Lists of sins are finite. They deal with individual issues that seem important in the moment but have minimal importance when compared with the all-encompassing and on-going issue of our relationships with others and with God.

Zeroing in on any particular moral issue gives that issue more importance than it deserves. It is not that we should be unconcerned with those things that challenge the harmony God wills for our lives, but it misses the point of how to keep our part of the Divine-human relationship on a harmonious level. When any list of sins is held out to force someone else to conform to the "righteous" understandings and outlook of another person, that list not only takes on more importance than it should have, it also denies God the divine right of offering peace and harmony ... the original intent of Creation.

Whenever any individual elevates himself to the point of believing they have the right and duty to "play God" by establishing what is proper for the lives of everyone else, that individual is living in a state of sin. The same can be said of any religious institution that attempts to do the same thing. History is a continuous witness to this fact. Despite the good intentions of individuals and organized religion to make the world a better place, when they overstep their bounds and deal with moral issues as if they were the end-all of establishing harmony, they sin. They sin because often their efforts end up breaking the harmony and the relationships they sought to strengthen in the first place. So, what can be done?

First, every person has the obligation to understand himself as being limited by his human abilities. The same is true for religious organizations. It is not enough to acknowledge that we are human and that we can err. That only gives "lip service" to the obvious. The adage "actions speak louder than words" holds true for this discussion. We cannot just say these words and then set ourselves up as being superior to give us the "right" to judge or control others.

Next, we need to recognize and celebrate the second greatest gift God has given humanity. For the Christian, God's greatest gift was that of the life and death, the example and sacrifice, of Jesus the Christ. For everyone, Christian or not, God's second greatest gift is the gift to live life with a perfect freedom to think, say, and do what we want, to the end that we might fulfill our potential, becoming what we were created to be. That gift has been lost in a number of ways for some, but it is still a God-given hope and right for each person. Unless we acknowledge this truth, we are destined to continue down the same path that has been trod before, and we will continue to make the same mistake of trying to replace God in our attempts to regulate and control others. The relationship we are to have with those around us is not a Divine-human relationship. It is a relationship that cherishes the idea that we, and all others in the world, are in life's adventure together and that the only One who has the right to mold us in the divine image is God alone.

Third, given this second point, we need to see how we can make ourselves better to help others become better persons as well. The relationship game we play with others must be played on a level playing field. The rules of play must be the same rules we would apply to others. A life lived with humility, compassion, understanding, and graciousness is the only life worth living. Unless this is true, the whole life and example of Jesus was wasted for the Christian. Those who belong to other major religions can find within their set of beliefs a similar force for good. The God Force moves on, encouraging and enabling each person to respond in ways that strengthen and support others to become the persons they were meant to be … persons with the potential of mirroring the good we recognize in God.

Finally, even though the concept of living in sin is of ultimate importance, as is the concept of overcoming sin, it is imperative that we "chill out," as the modern vernacular would phrase it. Being human, means we have an important task to accomplish. That task is hard, but it is possible to achieve. The task is that we are to live in ways that develop and foster positive and healthy relationships that strengthen and support others. That task includes doing those things that lay the groundwork which will improve the conditions and enable the possibilities others may have in making the world a better place to live.

The divine Will does not call us to carry out the mission properly reserved for God. We are asked only to fulfill our human potential. When we naively understand God's mission to be our mission, it is time to take a step back to regroup. We are not judge and jury for anyone else—only for ourselves. When we get sidetracked and believe that we have been given the mission to "clean up" the world by imposing our wills and standards on others, we miss the whole purpose God had in creating us in the first place. We are called to live in an imperfect world as imperfect persons but with the potential to become more perfect in God's sight. We have been created to be fully human, not to be divine. We are called to meet our human potential by lifting and supporting others in their life struggles. To assume that we can overcome the limitations that come with being human is a futile exercise. It is important that we live in a way that reflects the image of God, but that doesn't mean that we can be like God, nor should we strive to that end.

We are who we are. We are called to let God be God. If we judge by history, accepting those two truths has proven to be next to impossible. The struggle to attain our full human potential is a noble calling, indeed. The only way that calling can be accomplished is by recognizing and accepting our place in God's universe. When that is accomplished, we are as close to becoming the image of God that is possible. Until that happens, we live in the state of sin. We are sinners, not because of the things we do but because of our state of being.

If all this is true, then we are faced with the need to improve our relationships with others. The drive to make others conform to any individual's understanding of what they should be must be expunged from the normal human *modus operandi*. At first, it would seem to be an impossible undertaking. It can be accomplished, though, if as that drive is controlled a different drive is nurtured to take its place. Instead, of concentrating on making the other person better by berating that person for being the way he is, it is more god-like to help that person see the potential he has in life.

Both individuals and groups find ways to do this. Most often this happens in times of stress and turmoil. The times we best reflect our human potential are the times when we come to the aid of others in their darkest hour. A core aspect of our humanity is the awareness of the limitations we all have to deal with life as it impinges upon us. Responding to this awareness is almost an unconscious drive, but it is as natural as anything can be. Think of all the times we hear of the devastation faced by others who have experienced natural disasters. Now think of how we respond. Aid is sent. Volunteers assemble to rebuild physical structures ... homes, schools, churches, hospitals, and the like. Others respond to rebuild the emotional and psychological well-being of those who are suffering. The same thing happens when someone experiences personal loss. Friends, co-workers, classmates, acquaintances from the past and even some who don't have close ties with the one who is suffering find ways to express their sympathy and offer condolence. It's a natural thing to do on those occasions of turmoil. It can become more natural a thing to do in the everyday ordinary experiences of life, too.

Deep within us is the desire to be like God. A problem surfaces when some try to replace God by exercising the freedom they have been given, but doing so is part of the human condition. We can answer that desire in positive ways. Every person has the opportunity and the potential, no matter how hidden it may be, to be humble, compassionate, understanding, and gracious. When those attributes are expressed in thought and deed a person finally becomes the image of God he was meant to be. The state of sin is broken. The relationship that was meant to be between God and ourselves and others is achieved, and we live in a state of grace.

How we view sin and how we view grace determines how we see and understand God. When all the negative potentials of life take precedence in our evaluation of others and when we concentrate on the ways others fall prey to being human, then we hold an image of God that is judgmental and vindictive. We entertain an image of a God who is just waiting for us to make a mistake so that we can be punished, even to the point of eternal damnation.

When the positive potential in life takes precedence in our evaluation of others and when we concentrate on the ways others meet their human potential, then we hold an image of God that is forgiving and nurturing. We entertain an image of a God who celebrates the way we relate to others, setting the tone for an eternal reward.

This leaves us with two questions. The first is which God is more appealing and is this the God we want to follow and adore? The second question is if sin is not a list of wrongs but is, instead, a state of being, what do we do about the good and the bad things in life? The next chapter begins to answer those questions.

Before going on let us review the two concepts that are the basis for this chapter. We must let God be God, and we must accept who we are with our separate human strengths and weaknesses. We are who we are. God and our experiences and relationships have made us so. Being able to accept this truth is the first step toward fulfilling the potential God sees in us. We become better persons by concentrating on the things we can correct in ourselves. We do not become better by concentrating on the things that are wrong with others. We become instruments of God when we are willing to work to better ourselves so that we can come closer to meeting our own potential. When this happens the problem of sin disappears, and the world moves on toward God's original intent.

Premise of Chapter Eight

The Nature of Good and Evil is a moral and ethical issue and does not define sin.

CHAPTER 8

"The Nature of Good and Evil"

**Let us therefore no longer pass judgment
on one another, but resolve instead never to
put a stumbling block or hindrance in the
way of another. I know and am persuaded
in the Lord Jesus that nothing is unclean in
itself; but it is unclean for anyone who thinks
it unclean ... So, do not let your good be
spoken of as evil ... Let us then pursue what
makes for peace and for mutual up-building.**

Romans 14:13-14, 16, 19

THEOLOGICALLY SPEAKING, IF all the things we have grown used to calling sins are not sin, then what are they? A corollary question is, if we understand some things to be inherently bad, wrong, or evil, are there other things by nature that seem inherently good, right, and virtuous ... and how do they fit into the discussion of sin as presented in the last chapter?

Religious groups and individuals have tried to simplify the concept of sin and its impact on humanity. Their attempt to clarify the nature of the Divine-human relationship has evolved in such a way as to concentrate on the things that seem to cause a break in that relationship rather than concentrating on the relationship itself. As a result, the idea of what constitutes sin has changed.

It is to the credit of these religious groups and individuals that they attempted to simplify a terribly difficult concept, but the result is that our present understandings about sin and its corollary, virtue, have been watered down. As a result, the concept both of "sin" and "virtue" have assumed a lesser position theologically. By concentrating on what is perceived as the sinful act rather than the break that act causes in the Divine-human relationship, the impact of sin is marginalized.

A life well lived is a life that ties our very existence to God. Life lived with a strained relationship with God is not life at all. Individual "sinful" acts are not the final determination of how close a relationship we have with God, because God always chooses to deepen the Divine-human connection by forgiving all the things that keep us apart from each other and from God. This is another way of saying that God's act of Creation was not a one-time grand event, but is an act that continues today. Just as the physical universe expands and evolves, so does our psychological, emotional, and religious universe evolve. Every human being has been a part of God's ongoing act of creation, not just because new life has been given but also because the life of every individual has the potential of extending God's creative force through what they say and do. Each person builds on the influence of every person who has preceded him.

No person is a pawn in the game of life. The Divine Force has bequeathed the power of Creation to every individual, and it will be true for everyone who is yet to be born. Because of this, keeping lists of good and bad and right and wrong is a worthless endeavor. That effort centers on the past, and what has happened cannot be changed. It is in the here and now that change can take place. It is in the here and now that the Divine Force can continue its influence through humanity. The only possible positive purpose for keeping track of the good and bad acts of the past is that the remembrance of those acts may shine a corrective light on possible future actions. However, even this is problematic in that the past situations in which those acts were committed can never be replicated exactly. The situations and individuals that influence any given act are in a constant state of change. Therefore, the proper course of action never can be totally clear, and the outcome of any given act never can be known with certainty. The physical, social, psychological, and religious universe in which human beings exist is always changing. The attempt to apply finite rules to an infinitely changing world is futile. We can make certain assumptions as to the outcome of any given act, based on the past, but an assumption is not the same as certainty.

The human animal has evolved in such a manner so as to live by choice. Every individual has the power to decide what he or she will do in any given situation. Every day everyone is faced with myriad choices as to how to respond to life's issues and situations. In the chapter about sin, God's second greatest gift to humanity was identified as the gift of having a perfect freedom to be and act as that person chooses. Everyone, Christian or not, religious or not, has been given this gift. How this gift is used tells whether Creation will be advanced or will be hindered.

The only time period in which God's act of Creation can continue is the present with its own unique set of influences. What has happened cannot be changed, but what is happening can be refocused so that the Divine force of Creation can continue. But even with experience as a guide, one cannot be certain that any act is truly an act of Creation. Being able to discern the nature of things and deciding whether any individual act is good or bad does not come with an iron clad guarantee that we will be "right."

There is not and should not be any list of things that is absolute in human nature. The situation, itself, is a determining factor as to whether any individual act is good or bad. How others are affected and whether our relationship with the God Force is strengthened is the true test of our actions. The ongoing activity of God in Creation is inextricably woven in Grace. God's grace and forgiveness for the things we do that separate us from God sets the tone for a loving and endearing relationship with both God and humanity. Individual virtuous acts counter the "sinful" deeds we so often identify in our relationships with others. When one acts in a virtuous way, one mirrors the graceful activity of God, and it is then that the Divine-human relationship is made stronger.

This said, it is key to reaffirm the importance of life's situations in determining whether any individual act is sinful or virtuous. Some would question the idea that no human act is inherently good or bad. The evaluation of human action comes as those actions are interpreted considering the situation that surrounds them. We move from the theological discussion of sin and virtue to an ethical discussion of bad and good because of the interrelationship between the situation and the resulting acts taking place in response to the situation.

In the 1960's, Joseph Fletcher, then an Episcopal priest, turned the world of theologians upside down with his theory that there is no absolute law except the single idea that love, alone, is the determining factor as to how a person is to respond to his life situation. [NOTE: Joseph Fletcher, <u>Situation Ethics</u>...The New Morality, Louisville, KY: Westminster John Knox Press, 1966.] He maintained that the question "What is the most loving thing to do?" is the only question that needs to be answered when trying to determine a course of action in any given situation. Emulating *agape* love, the form of love we attribute to God, which is all consuming and all encompassing, absolute and unconditional, is necessary to provide direction for our lives.

Theologians of all persuasions challenged his contention. His postulate was contrary to the accepted idea that in life there is a set of rules or laws that, when violated, contradicted God's intent for life. Christian theologians and ethicists, and those of other faiths, argued that a moral and ethical life could be maintained only by following prescribed standards.

Fletcher's new approach to ethics challenged the weakness of mainstream ethical thought. For instance, the Commandment, "You shall not kill," always has had to be redefined by traditional theologians to separate the idea of murder from the idea of killing for some other "higher" value or reason. Traditionalists maintained that there had to be excusable exceptions to this Commandment. One was not to murder, but it was all right to kill an enemy combatant in war, or it was all right to kill someone in self-defense or to protect a loved one, never mind the fact that a life had been taken. Yet, in these situations both the traditionalists and Fletcher shared the need for allowing the act of killing. The traditionalist does so by looking at the "higher" value or reason for the act. Those who bought into Fletcher's moral interpretation allowed themselves an "out" by interpreting the action as being the most loving thing to do for the most persons affected by that action.

In the bioethical realm of today, Fletcher and traditional theologians would take umbrage with each other. Some traditionalists would consider the life of a mother to be expendable to save the life of an unborn fetus, if that were the only way to protect the "most innocent" of the two parties. Or, in the case of a patient enduring chronic and debilitating pain without hope for a cure, some traditionalists would argue to maintain the patient's painful existence in opposition to Fletcher's stand that it would be most loving to withdraw medication (or perhaps, even administer medication) to allow the patient to expire as early as possible, giving final relief to the patient and providing the patient's family with greater physical resources and psychological peace.

Fletcher was famous for using extreme examples to support his postulate that love alone should be the determining factor for deciding the proper course of action. He hypothesized a story of a family taken prisoner by the Nazis in the Second World War. The mother and father were separated from each other and from their children, and all were sent to concentration camps. Somehow the father was released and spent all his efforts looking for his children, and after finding them, obtaining their release. They were reunited and were a strong support for each other. However, the mother remained a prisoner. Fletcher continued by presenting the character of a sympathetic Prison Commandant, who explained to the mother that if she became pregnant, she might be released as being inferior, no longer able to carry her load of work. The mother felt the possibility for freedom was better than her present situation, so she sought out a guard willing to impregnate her. He did. She was released. Eventually, the mother was reunited with her family, and after explaining her miraculous release she introduced her newborn to the family. Her husband and her other children accepted the mother back and welcomed the new child into the family. They offered unconditional love, and all involved were better off for having strengthened their relationships with one another, emulating God's Grace, forgiveness and welcoming nature. Fletcher used such examples to bolster his "new morality," and his work was not only hotly debated but also dismissed by many.

There are many reasons why Fletcher's "new morality" has not taken root in Christian and other religious moral thinking, but Fletcher did open the door for discussion and ethical exploration. In the decades since Fletcher first postulated his theory of ethics, based on the single imperative of *agape* love, society in general continually has been more open to his thoughts than many who claim to be trained theologians. Social issues such as abortion, mercy killing, premarital sex, divorce, single-parent impregnation and/or parenting, same-sex marriage, and other less volatile issues such as having two wage earners in a family or having a family with the woman as the wage earner and the man as the house-husband have been gaining popular support without the blessing of the more traditional theologians and ethicists. In fact, this has happened in the face of outright opposition from those traditionalists.

Does this popular support make it right? Are the traditionalists helping or hindering the movement toward more liberal ethical thinking? Are ethical issues reshaping political concerns, or are political concerns reshaping ethical thinking? Only time will tell.

The social issues of our day may seem ultimate in importance, but they are not! No matter how hard the battle is waged over these things, they do not get to the heart of the question the traditionalists or Fletcher, himself, have been trying to decide. The traditionalists have missed the point by dealing with these issues as being sinful. Fletcher missed the point by emphasizing *agape* love as being the cure-all for life's problems. Perhaps a new way of thinking would be more to the point.

To this end, we first must attempt to discount all those things that have been identified as being sin. We must re-categorize them. Remember, sin is a state of being. It is the condition of living, separated from God. Sin is not any of those things we keep lists of, which we, or others, may commit ... bad though they may be.

Next, we must avoid the trap in Fletcher's postulate. The attempt to understand both sin and the reality of normal human good and bad acts must be kept separate. Fletcher understood that the Divine-human relationship was paramount in determining the nature of sin. He saw love as the ultimate test of healing relationships, and felt that doing the most loving thing for the most people involved in any given situation was the key to helping persons come to their full potential. Given this understanding, Fletcher advanced ethical thought more than most others have done in centuries. But, despite this, he missed the mark by identifying *agape* love as the final answer to ethical issues.

The last step is to take Fletcher's work and substitute the importance of the Divine-human relationship for his emphasis on *agape* love. If the Divine-human relationship is the target of our thinking, then the issue of living an ethical life becomes clearer. Persons come closer to God when their relationship with God is the focal point of their actions. The question should not be, "What is the most loving thing to do?" but "How will my actions bring me (and others) closer to God?" "How will what I do move me closer to fulfilling the potential God sees in me?" Answering those questions not only emphasizes the love aspect of Fletcher's postulate; it also makes us aware of our continual connection to God and how that connection can bind us more strongly to one another.

Fletcher tells us, "We ought to love people and use things. The essence of immorality is that we use people and love things." These few words get to the heart of Fletcher's new morality. They set the tone for deepening the relationships we have with each other and with God for they point us beyond simple moral and ethical action.

To satisfy ourselves with the idea that sin is simply an immoral act allows us to escape the reality of true sin. Sin is any thought, word, or deed that builds a barrier between ourselves and others, and as a result, between ourselves and God. Everyday acts, whether they are good or bad, have moral or ethical consequences. They affect the well-being of others, and, therefore, are important in the collection of everyday life experiences. But doing good things or practicing evil count as virtue or sin only so far as those actions build or break the Divine-human relationship. Otherwise, they are simply negative or positive acts. Myriad examples can help to differentiate moral or ethical acts from sin. The "sins" any individual chooses to identify will depend on his experience and the influence others have had in creating his value system.

For example, for most people, singing in church is not a sin, but for a minority, singing in church is sinful. Some consider having a picture taken of them to be a sin, because it is an act of vanity. Most don't. Some believe that the use of modern energy sources is sinful, but most individuals see this as arcane and of little consequence. A growing number of persons believe that eating meat is not only unhealthful, but is sinful, because it requires the life of the animals that are slaughtered; or that it is sinful because it may contribute to a variety of unhealthful physical conditions. It is a minority opinion. But does that mean the opinion is wrong? Is it a moral issue, or a sin, to eat meat? Such examples seem trivial to most, but to those who hold these beliefs they are very important. Still, the distinction must be made. Are these things sins, or are they questions of morality?

Making the distinction between sin and morality becomes more difficult when any issue affects the well-being of others in a more direct way. Take the issue of veganism. Eating meat may or may not be a sin, theologically speaking. If choosing not to eat meat does not affect the relationship the vegan has with others, and therefore by implication it does not affect the relationship the vegan has with God, then it is not a sin. The opposite is also true. If someone chooses to eat meat and this does not affect their relationship with one who is vegan, then it is not a sin. But, in either case, it would be a sin if the choice to eat or not to eat meat causes turmoil among family or friends. If arguments about whether it is sinful to eat meat break out in the kitchen, or at the dinner table, or when thoughts spring up about the "stupidity" of those who choose not to eat meat, or when thoughts of "mindless cruelty" are applied to the meat-eater, then sin is present. No wonder we find it easier to identify sin as an act, rather than a relationship builder/destroyer. Even though the easy route may seem better, is it really? If choosing to eat meat or not affected only the individual who believes the act is right or wrong, life would be so much easier. The same could be said about all the other opinions of those with whom we come in contact. The theological truth remains, that when what we think or do causes a break in our relationship (human or divine), those activities are sin. And when what we think or do does not cause a breakdown in our relationships, those things are not sin. They simply are moral or immoral acts and attitudes. They are no more than our opinion of what is right or wrong, what is good or bad.

The reader must decide what the most compelling thing is, when dealing with moral and ethical issues. Is it most important to judge the individual actions and attitudes of others as being sinful or virtuous? Or is it more important to deal with others in ways that allow for growth of understanding and compassion for those who may be making choices that seem to be harmful and hurtful?

Acts of grace always trump judgmental attitudes when dealing with things theologically. Determining what is right and good is a noble goal, worthy of our best efforts, but it is not the most important thing to consider. Accepting this fact is the first step toward fulfilling the potential God has created in everyone. Methodists have learned this is what their founder, John Wesley, had in mind when he said, "we are to go on to perfection." He wasn't fooling himself when he said that. He had no illusions as to the ability of anyone to become "perfect," but it was the hope and goal he believed God had set for everyone. When human efforts mirror the graceful and forgiving nature of the Divine Force, sin moves from the forefront and is replaced by the harmony God intended, as depicted in the story of the Garden of Eden when Adam and Eve were living in unity with God. But more of that later in the chapter on "How to Read the Bible."

Premise for Chapter Nine

A new concept of "Life after Death," needs to be formulated, that is less mystical and more palatable to contemporary thought in Western society.

CHAPTER 9

"Eternal Life"

**"...and if I die before I wake,
I pray the Lord my soul to take."**

**--Joseph Addison, "The
Spectator," March 8, 1711**

SEVERAL FORCES DRIVE people to practice religion. Many of the mysteries of life can be answered for some only by the way their religion explains those mysteries. Most of the time those explanations go beyond logical reasoning, and we fall back on the answer most given by the Church when confronted by lack of logical proof ... "You must take it on faith." It is a circular thought process that for some is worthless, for some is comforting, and for others, compelling. Questions about the possibility of eternal life and about the reality of heaven and hell relate to two of the forces that drive persons to religious belief.

The children's prayer snippet that appears above is an example of how even the prayers we make early in our lives contribute to our theological understandings. We become the persons we are because of the impact of our experiences and the relationships we have, as we grow to maturity. Our prayers, our concept of sin, our thoughts about good and evil, our image of heaven and hell, and our concept of eternal life all help to establish our theological understandings and outlook.

We wonder, what is heaven like? Where do we go for all eternity? There must be more to existence than a final stop in a cemetery. We ponder the end of our lives and hope that there is something more that lies before us. It is this hope, or the fear that nothing lies ahead, or the fear of what lies ahead, that drives us to believe in the mystery of an "after-life." After all, what good is religion, if there is no reward at the end of life?

If we believe that "God is Good," or that "God is Love," then there must be more at the end of our existence than the plot of ground we will inhabit, surrounded by others who have died. We reason that because we have done our best, God has something more planned for us ... a life that exceeds the life we are living in this present world. Whether life has been hard or has been filled with rewards, we cling to the hope that there is something better for us that lies ahead.

That hope fills the hearts and minds of all religious people, no matter the depth of their faith, no matter what faith group it is they claim as their own. Most persons who claim to be a part of an organized religion ... Christians, Muslims, Jews, those who practice oriental religions, and even those who practice native earth religions ... hold a common belief that there is something else in store for them at the end of their earthly existence. The same is true for those who claim spirituality as their faith expression [NOTE: This refers to those who base their religious understandings on subjective experience and psychological growth as opposed to traditional religious development combined with the social/psychological theme of this book]. Common to the human experience is the need to feel that there is more to life than residence in the ground, or on a mantle in an urn, once their time walking the earth has expired.

The human experience has not changed much over the ages. Even before the existence of organized religion, there was a common need for the comfort of having the promise of an eternal life. We began our thoughts with the story of Aboguli and his clan. We've looked at the impact of those who claimed mythological faith expressions and understandings, as we considered the Gilgamesh Epic and the similar story of Noah and the Ark. We've briefly reviewed some of the important Christian theologians who have helped form our faith through the centuries. And we have our own experiences and relationships to support our faith understandings. All this leads us to believe that as part of the mix of divine creation there is more to life than an end that culminates in nothingness.

Still, our thoughts about heaven and hell and eternal life can be quite different. What we imagine is determined by the way our experience has influenced us. Our personal attitudes about these things (and about everything else) are unique unto ourselves. The

Dynamic Force we call God has provided us with the ability to create an understanding of things eternal that can satisfy our human need for the assurance that life can go on, even after our final breath has left. Because we are unique and because our individual experiences and our relationships are different, it is logical that everyone will create a vision of things eternal that is unique. It cannot be a universal vision for everyone. So, here too, we find another mindset that can and often does create contention among believers of different faiths and even believers within a single faith.

As we pursue our discussion of the concept of heaven, hell, and the after-life, we will limit our thoughts to Christian perspectives. But the Muslim, the Jew, the Buddhist and those holding other religious beliefs all have a common need to envision what lies beyond the grave.

For some Christians, the first image that occurs is the barrier they see as limiting admission to heaven. Saint Peter controls each person's entry as he stands his post at the "Pearly Gates." Armed with volumes of reports on each applicant seeking admission, Saint Peter becomes the ultimate authority as to whether each person is worthy of the reward of eternal life in the company of God. This image is most important to those who understand their earthly life, and the lives of those they judge, as being a "testing ground" for their "saintliness." They ask: "Are we worthy of reward for our struggles against evil and our aspirations of good." This understanding affects not only themselves but it influences others, as well

... even those who may not be as concerned about their "rightful" admission to heaven.

This second group may not have as deep a concern about their eternal reward as they go about their everyday activities and be less bound by the constraints of righteous living on a daily basis. Still, when they find themselves facing imminent death, they question whether their lives were, indeed, good enough to go on to heaven.

Because of their background, there are still others who claim a belief in God, but do not exercise their freedom to express that belief in their everyday living, including participation in a faith grouping. These persons may have a vague or ill-defined concept of God. Their concept limits their ability not only to define God, but it limits also the concept they hold of themselves as being part of the Divine Force. These Christians have never experienced a meaningful divine-human relationship, or if they have, they have opted out of that relationship. Because of this, their idea of an after-life and their vision of heaven and hell necessarily will be vague, too. Still, this group of Christians influences the understandings and beliefs of others.

Another group of Christians are even less concerned with whether they will be admitted to heaven and what the after-life is about. They understand that the God who provided for their welfare and comfort throughout their lives would be a God of gracious acceptance into heaven. They enjoy the certainty that the love they already have experienced will be a love continued beyond the barrier of the grave. These persons, too, affect others.

Finally, some Christians understand God's love sufficiently to be completely satisfied with the life they have been given, even if that life experience has been less than perfect. They can rest in peace even if death is really the end of their divine-human relationship. They can be comfortable in the knowledge that no conscious harm will ever come to them. They appreciate what they have already experienced, knowing that the life they have had is not of their own making, but is a gift from God, and they relish the gifts they have already been given. The full appreciation of the things they have enjoyed in life is enough for them. Their concern is less for the unknown future than it is for experiencing the present.

The possibility or probability of an after-life and the form that after-life takes varies with the individual. The understanding one has of the nature of heaven and/or hell is determined more by the influences life has had on an individual than it does on a concrete reality. Once death comes and an individual passes from the realm of the living, as we know it, the future will be what the future will be. No one lies on his deathbed able to see with certainty what lies ahead.

Each individual or faith grouping may have a part of the truth when trying to envision and understand the possibility of an after-life. Their truth depends on their individual or collective musings, as influenced by the thoughts of others. No one's vision can be summarily dismissed because it doesn't conform to another person's vision. A dogmatic position about the nature of our eternal future has no claim on anyone except the one who holds that position. The visions we have of heaven and eternity cannot be molded into a one-size-fits-all vision.

If this is true, what is left? Is the hope of eternity with God just a dream? If so, what is the point of trying to live in a way that is worthy of becoming a part of the heavenly host?

Most persons want to believe that life does not end with death. When another person claims to have had an after-death experience, many rush to listen. They seize upon the latest tale of walking through a dark tunnel into a brilliant light of peace and understanding. They revel in the possibility of the reports of those who have been brought back from death, and who have witnessed the last-ditch efforts of others to save them on the operating table. Some can't get enough of the stories of those who have envisioned Jesus reaching out to them and taking them into "a place of peace," only to return to tell of the experience. The persons who relish these stories, more than any other persons, represent the hope that dwells within most everyone that there is something more to life beyond the grave. They are willing to grasp for the possibility of that life through the experiences and expressions of others.

But why rely on, or at least hope, that the experiences of others give proof of God's love? Can anyone really provide for others the kind of guarantee that is sought to fill our innermost human need ... to be at one with a Power that promises to transcend our earthly limitations? This need is universal. It is not limited to those who are religious. It exists as an integral part of the human psyche.

Some may seem not to be concerned with an after-life. They go about their everyday activities taking power over others and over the life situations they can affect; but the power they possess is an illusion. In the end, when faced with death, every person has the need to believe that there is more than what has gone before. It is then that they begin to weigh their lives to see if they have been worthy of the promise that the Christ has offered. I contend that this is true even for those who see the grave as their end-point. But, like so many things religious, this cannot be proved.

There is another possibility that could apply to all persons, no matter what their concept of an after-life might be. As we consider that possibility, we must consider all the many and varied concepts each of the groups described above hold as a tenant of their faith.

A basic theological understanding is the idea that even though our human existence has finite limits, God is not finite. God is assumed to have existed even before Creation. The Divine Force is credited with the power to have made all that has been made. And that Divine Force continues its efforts of creation in the everyday life and experiences we enjoy. We further reason that the Divine Force will continue after our existence has ended. That is why we understand God to be an Everlasting God.

The whole concept of an after-life is an unconscious effort to extend human existence into the realm of the divine. One of the points of the story of Adam and Eve is that as humans we seek to be more god-like. We want to know what is good and what is evil. We want the power God has without the limits that human existence puts on us. We want to live forever … just like God. All these things, and more, will be covered in the chapter on how to read the Bible.

If nothing but God is everlasting, how can anyone hope for an eternal life? All the traditional visions of heaven and/or hell rely on believing that there exists another place, a parallel universe, so to speak, where we go once we have left this life. We start with the pearly gates, walk on streets paved with gold, live with those we love who have gone before. We find hope that the good relationships we have enjoyed will be even better once we have claimed the zip code of heaven. Or the opposite is true. We lose hope, if we have lived despicable lives, and we fear that the warmth of our surroundings will be unbearable. Rainbows or pitchforks—that is heaven or hell. We find comfort in the idea that even our best imaginings cannot do justice to what the after-life will be like. We know that whatever it is like, it will exceed our hopes and dreams. That is heaven. We dread the idea that if we have failed to meet God's expectations, the after-life will be worse than anything we can imagine. That is hell.

Return to the idea that only God is eternal. What does that do to the concept of an eternal life in heaven or hell? Are there really two eternal things, the first being God and the second being life in places called reward and punishment? The idea that we can live eternally runs counter to the concept that we are finite beings. We have been created as beings dependent on God. It seems blasphemous to claim that there is a way to be like God in the sense we will exist forever. It is hard to reconcile our previous understandings of an eternal God, when we embrace the concept of life eternal for ourselves. It makes our concept of God's everlasting nature seem less important, when we co-opt that nature, given our human limitations.

The Roman Catholic Church has added a third state of existence beyond the grave. It holds that there is heaven and hell ... and purgatory. Of all the doctrine and teaching of the Roman Catholic Church, the concept of purgatory stands as one of the most controversial. The Church maintains that the idea of purgatory has both biblical and traditional support. Protestant groups have long challenged the idea of purgatory, and history attests to the unrest the concept has engendered. The Orthodox and Roman branches of Catholicism hold differing views of purgatory, as well. Why?

What is Purgatory? The Church maintains that it is a transitional state in which those who have died await final acceptance into heaven, so they can enjoy the full benefits of life everlasting in the presence of God. The Church argues that at death everyone has vestiges of sin that need to be stripped away, even though God has already afforded them forgiveness. It is a period for purification rather than simply a "holding" place in which those who have died await their final reward.

A part of being human is the fact that everyone has been given the freedom to think, say, and do things that will either bring them closer to the Divine Force or will create a barrier between themselves and God. It is human nature for everyone to have chosen unwisely at times. Because, on occasion, all persons act in a way that separates them from God, the Roman Catholic Church has devised a way for those who are living to intercede on behalf of those who have died. The Church has labored to explain that there is a hierarchy of sin that defines the gravity of the separation from God that many have imposed on themselves. It is understood that God seeks to be at one with all of Creation, and therefore it is the duty of the Church to help bridge the separation that has been created. The Church maintains that there is hope, because the vestiges of sin can be removed, so that only the essential good nature of the person, who has died, remains. Because of this doctrinal understanding, purgatory moves from being a simple concept to one that is laden with enough minutiae to change the nature of sin in a multitude of ways.

Any time a concept is challenged, the arguments defending that concept are subject to a variety of explanations and alterations. Some of these arguments are subtle and some not so subtle; and some of the conclusions the Church now holds are different from what were first put forth. Even a long-held belief that has become established dogma can rightfully face challenge.

What troubles most modern theologians who argue against the concept of purgatory, is the underlying idea that God offers forgiveness to those who are repentant, but that God's forgiveness seems to have limits. The idea of purgatory implies that to be forgiven completely, a soul needs time to garner the necessary attributes to be worthy of a place in God's divine arena of everlasting life. What does this idea do to the belief that God is all-powerful and all-forgiving? Does God need the Church to provide the added security of this transitional period to "shape up" God's potential neighbors for eternity?

A second and equally troubling point about the concept of purgatory is the idea that the Church can actually do things for those who have died. It is a proper right and duty of the Church to affirm God's forgiving nature. But is it proper for the Church to claim the need for and means of purification of the soul? Is not God's willingness to accept a person into the heavenly realm enough? If God is already satisfied that those who have died have fully completed "the race," as the apostle Paul describes our span on earth, then why is there any necessity for the Church to offer a "second and final chance" to become worthy of eternal life? The Church offers those who have been left behind the means of "helping" their loved ones attain the glory of life everlasting in the presence of God. The assistance they offer under the guidance of the Church through their prayers, petitions, and the giving of alms takes from God what God has already claimed ... the right to forgive fully those whom God has created.

There IS a positive aspect to the idea that we can offer ourselves up to God on behalf of those whom we love. If the concept of purgatory has any merit, it rests in the fact that it recognizes and emphasizes the connection between the living and the dead, a connection that cannot be broken, a connection that can continue the process of creation, which transcends even the grave. It is a benefit to the living to believe that, in returning the love they have enjoyed through the lives of those who have died, they reflect the true meaning of the love and friendship they have received. But this is a benefit reaped by the living, not by those who have died. If purgatory is understood in this way, then God retains the power only the Almighty has the right to wield. It eliminates the underlying idea that the Church as a whole and we as individuals hold the power to mitigate the sin of those who have died. It also helps to emphasize the importance of all relationships, and it opens the door to the idea that we can affect others and build better connections with them. But it is best to exert our energies to that end on the living, not the dead.

It would be easy to be sidetracked in our discussion of eternal life by arguments about purgatory. So, let us return to the central idea of what eternal life is like. There is only one thing that is eternal. It is the essence of God. It is the Divine Force that has existed even before the world was established. It is this Force that will continue even beyond the end of time. If this is true, what does this do to the whole idea of heaven and hell?

Can it be that eternal life does not continue in an external place, a place we have created in our minds that we call heaven or hell? The creation of those eternal "kingdoms" comes from the desire to explain how it is that a relationship with God can be continued, even beyond the grave. We understand that we can enjoy God's unlimited goodness in the here and now, and we cling to the hope that that goodness will continue in an unknown future.

It does continue, but it continues not in an external and eternal place, separate from God. It continues within the God Force, itself. Life eternal can be for us an eternity lived even closer to God than the idea heaven provides. Eternal life is lived in the "mind and memory" of God. Eternal life is not residence in a place called heaven or hell. At first glance this may seem preposterous, especially to those long schooled in the idea of a "heavenly place." But don't we already say that "We can be at one with God" when we do those things that seem to further God's kingdom here on earth? Don't we already maintain, "We are one with God," when we follow the example of Jesus? If we make these claims to be at one with God in the here and now, why is it strange to believe that we can be at one with God dwelling in God's divine essence? The union with God that is hoped for is more fully and completely attained, if after death God accepts our lives as they were created. What we have done with those lives rests in the Divine memory of God and that remembrance becomes our final resting place and therefore continues for all eternity.

In the first account of Creation in Genesis, the one that talks about God forming the heavens, the earth, and all that exists (not the story that tells about Adam and Eve), one of the important points comes near the end of the tale. After God created humankind in God's own image and everything was declared to be good, the man and the woman were given dominion over everything God had made. From the beginning, God intended that man and woman would be full partners with God for all eternity. This story of Creation tells that human life is different from the life of all other living things. God's crowning act of creation was the making of persons who could live in relationship with each other and with God. Humankind was created with a special potential that enabled everyone to participate in the creative force of God. A partnership was established in which humankind became a part of this force of creation. That partnership extends beyond the limits of our earthly life into the realm of the eternal. The grave does not mark the end, for God remembers and celebrates the good we have done during our earthly lives, and God carries that memory on for all eternity.

We already have experienced the joy of deep relationships with others. We can enjoy a similar deep and underlying relationship with God. At the same time, we enhance our relationships with others, we enhance our relationship with the Divine Force. These two acts are not separate; they are entwined. When Jesus shared what we refer to as the Great Commandment in Matthew 22:37b-40, he revealed this truth. Loving God and loving our neighbor as our self may seem to be two separate acts, but they are not. When this is understood, it takes our relationships to a higher level. "Truly, I say to you, as you did it to one of the least of these, my brethren, you did it to me," said Jesus, as recorded in Matthew 25:40b. These two passages from Matthew hold the key to God's celebration and judgment of our actions. What we have done and what we do constitute our eternal existence. The mind and memory of God hold us in God's heart for eternity.

There is a tangible benefit for us in the here and now, if eternal life is understood to be lived in the "mind and memory" of God. Our human relationships take on deeper meaning. They are not just everyday occurrences that allow for limited involvements. They become much more than that. If God is going to be eternally aware and involved in our relationships with others in each life experience, then would we not be more inclined to do the "godly" thing and be more loving, accepting, and forgiving to those we meet? The everlasting connection with God is emphasized more fully when we see our everyday involvements as being a part of God's eternal relationship with us.

We can understand God more completely when we claim the possibility of eternity, not just as neighbors of God in heaven, but as an integral part of the Divine Force, itself. If God gives us the ultimate gift of being a part of the Divine essence, we can finally claim the nature of being at one with God. It is easier to know the Unknowable when we are a part of the Unknowable. God is no longer an Incognito God, One who is hidden or disguised. God becomes fully revealed and because of that the peace we seek is granted.

Finally, because we claim the gift God offers to become a part of the Divine Force, all the limitations we experience as humans are removed after we die. We no longer need to think or do anything on our own. We are not constrained in any way, for we no longer limit God's call upon us, as we assume our place in God's heart, mind, and memory … a gift that has always been offered to us. That simply is another way of saying, "we are transformed."

A basic assertion of this book is that everyone is a theologian. This means we do not need to borrow the concepts of others as to what God is like or how we can relate to God. Our relationships and experiences have made us who we are. Therefore, this author's idea of eternal life need not become your idea. But each time a new concept about life and life everlasting is considered, every person has a new option with which to deal. The mere consideration of new possibilities makes everyone a bit different. We change when confronted with different ideas. Sometimes we change by adopting and adapting the ideas of others and incorporating those ideas into our own thoughts. Other times we change by reinforcing previously held ideas. You, the reader, are free to decide what seems important and truthful for yourself.

This new understanding of what eternal life with God might be like has an added benefit. It enables us to be a part of the ongoing process of Creation, as we say and do things that recognize the goodness in those around us and in those who have gone before us. We accentuate the positive, not because it will help us gain a reward, but because the process brings us closer to God.

A basic tenant of Christianity is that "We live by faith, and we focus on the life to come." The concept of eternal life with God that has been proposed above emphasizes that goal. It ties the possibility of eternal life more completely to the lives we live daily. It breaks down the separation we make between life in the here and now and life everlasting. It provides the opportunity to make each contact with others more meaningful and important. It affords us the possibility of living more fully in harmony with those who surround us. It opens the door to the possibility of heaven on earth ... a life lived more harmoniously with God.

Premise of Chapter Ten

The elements of Contemporary Worship define the nature of God.

CHAPTER 10

"The Secularization of Worship"

"Let us turn to #57 in our Hymnals ... 'O for a Thousand Tongues to Sing'"

The United Methodist Hymnal

EVERYONE HAS A concept of God. Some rely on their experiences and relationships to form that theology. Some rely on the influence of the media, forming their beliefs on secular influences such as movies, TV evangelists, and news commentaries. Others let their moral compass guide them, and their concepts of what is right or wrong help them form their beliefs. Many cling to only the earliest learnings they experienced in Sunday school to express their theology and religious understandings. Some choose to emulate the ideas and actions of others whom they admire. Still others base their beliefs on the understandings of their church and the influence that comes from participation in church programs. Everyone combines these influences in some way, and an unending variety of theological understandings surface in any population.

There are many ways God chooses to be revealed to us. Any individual, atheist or agnostic, or a member of a Christian, Jewish, Muslim, Buddhist or other religious group, develops his own theology within the constraints of his own grouping. In this chapter, we will limit our examination of faith development to the Christian arena, especially to those who regularly attend church and participate in the activities their church offers. Even so, we must be aware that influences like those that impact the Christian in his faith grouping exist for the non-Christian in his own group.

When persons become a part of an organized religious group, they become indoctrinated with the overriding theology that group holds. The doctrine and religious expression of any religious group can take on a life of its own. Everything that group does impacts the individual's theological development and understanding. Two "Christian" groups, having extreme theological viewpoints, come to mind. The first is the KKK (Ku Klux Klan). It claims to be a Christian group but exhibits little similarity to most groups who claim to be Christian. An overriding influence on its membership is hate, not love. It considers some segments of society to be inferior and does its best to intimidate and subjugate those whom they cast as being evil and of less worth. The second group is Topeka's Westboro Baptist Church. It, too, claims to be a Christian group, but like the KKK, it denounces others who hold beliefs that are contrary to its own. It pickets churches and funerals of those who support gay and lesbian lifestyles, leaving little option for those whom they revile to be seen as children of God. Both groups are examples of how the religious mentality of their members can be molded into something quite different from generally accepted Christian understandings and expressions. All Christian religious groupings face the same forces that these extreme groups have encountered, but they have responded more openly and, as a result, are considered by most to be purer in their Christian doctrine and understandings.

Everything a religious group does within its scope of activity has an impact on the theology of its members. The prayer life of the group; the songs and hymns it sings; the way children are treated; the way women are incorporated into or excluded from leadership positions; the secular activities of the congregation; the political viewpoints of the group; the way rituals such as weddings, funerals, and baptisms are conducted; and even the design and décor of the places of worship all contribute in significant ways to the theology that is developed within the membership. The purpose of this chapter is to look briefly at each of these influences to shed additional light on the impact that common socio-religious activities have on the faith development of those who are part of a religious group.

A person's theology is shaped by the influence of his congregation. If the congregation sees the God to whom a prayer is addressed as being judgmental and vengeful, then its prayer will reflect fear. However, if the congregation sees the God to whom a prayer is addressed as loving and accepting, then its prayer will reflect joy. The collective understanding of the group intensifies the understanding of the individual.

The earlier chapter on prayer dealt mainly with the nature of prayer and the influence prayer has on the individual. The thoughts that follow pertain to the impact corporate prayer has in determining the theology of the individual. What was said earlier could be summarized in the following way. The act of prayer has several purposes. When people pray, they are elevated to a level that allows them to communicate with God. That is something quite different from the forms of communication people have with others. Communication between equals is different from communication with God in that it is a humbling process that enables individuals to see the contrast between our human shortcomings and God's divine nature. Prayer goes beyond expressing the need to talk with God. It encourages us to see that we have the right to do so. By praying, persons are moved from their earthly constraints into the freedom of God's special realm. Prayer moves us from our everyday concerns in a way that allows us to prepare for eternity.

Through the ritual of corporate prayer, we acknowledge the mystery and might of God, not just as individuals, but also as part of God's family of followers. Prayers uttered in the worship setting acknowledge the value of community and the importance of others to whom we belong. Two points come to mind in this respect.

First, community prayer (a better term than "unison prayer") plays an important part in helping us see the value the Divine-Force places on our lives. To say our prayers in "unison" implies merely that we are saying the words at the same time. But to say our prayers in "community" carries the added implication that we are not alone, that we are a part of God's family and that God values our connections and our relationships with others. Prayer in the worship setting sets the tone for our lives outside the walls of the church. These prayers take us a step beyond reciting rote phrases that loose part of their meaning with familiarity. They encourage us to think about the words we say, as we sit among those who have chosen to worship God in a way that mirrors the understandings of our life situation and the way the Divine Force moves with us through our lives. As this becomes more obvious, we find that our vision of God changes. The emphasis on community reveals the Divine desire for us to be at one with each other and with the Divine-Force, itself.

Second, we must be careful as to how we pray. This is true always, but is especially important in the worship setting. Take, for instance, the part of the service when the congregation is asked to pray silently as a part of the prayer ritual. If the worship leader invites the congregation to lift their hearts in silent prayer, giving thanks for their blessings and making petitions for their needs, and then gives the membership fifteen seconds or less to do so, what does that say about the importance of those silent prayers? The importance of the congregation being comfortable during the worship time is understandable, and an extended time of silent prayer makes many people uncomfortable. But, is that reason enough to short change the chance of praying to God, surrounded by friends and family, as we are given the opportunity to "pour out our souls"?

Sometimes God speaks to us most clearly in moments of silence. Moments of quiet reflection may be the best time to hear the divine voice of God.

We live in an era when we demand immediate gratification and swift resolution of desires. It is comfortable not to have to think deeply about things ... even prayer. So, we find ourselves content simply to go through the motions of praying. What does this do to our concept of God? Is God a Force that can be appeased with a nod to what we know is important; or is God due our time and attention? Our very image of God subtly changes as we offer token homage. Rather than ten or fifteen seconds for silent prayer, is not a full minute or two appropriate in silent recognition of our blessings, our needs, and our relationship with others and with God? A minute speeds by when we are in the company of others who are sharing a time of fun and fellowship. A minute stalls (seemingly forever), when we force ourselves to contemplate the meaning of our lives and our relationship with God. What do we want God to understand about our lives and us? How we pray reveals our true relationship with God, and it helps tailor our image of God.

Next, consider how music in worship affects our image of God. The songs, hymns, and music a group incorporates in its worship setting have a profound effect on the personal and corporate theology within that group. The power of music, even more than the prayer life of the congregation, may be responsible for the theological development of its members.

Even those groups that choose not to include music in their rituals demonstrate a theological understanding that is reflected in the lack of song in their religious lives. For most people, worship without song leaves a void. Without music, worship seems somber and sterile. Some of the joy of worship that exists for most individuals seems lacking when music is absent. When instrumental music is eschewed, the whole nature of the worship setting is different. Those who believe music is a distraction that keeps persons from concentrating on God's divine nature, argue that nothing should stand between God and the worshiper. For them, music is something that interferes with the closeness one could have simply by experiencing quiet meditation and solemn prayer. So, for some, shunning music is a way to come closer to God. It is a practice that opens the worshiper to silent contemplation. As a result, those who practice this kind of quiet reflection understand both God and life to be more austere in nature than most other persons do.

At the other end of the spectrum, there are persons and groups that derive much of their theological perspective from the music incorporated in their worship setting. Instrumental music plays a major role in their theological development. With the sounds of an organ penetrating the walls and reverberating through the corridors of grand churches and cathedrals, one is hard pressed not to envision a God of great magnitude and noble grandeur. The might and majesty of God cannot be missed when music envelops the worshiper. The soft sound of flute or clarinet, or violin and viola, in contrast to the magnitude of the organ, encourage worshippers to understand the more subtle, light, and calm nature of God.

But the songs and hymns sung in the worship setting have even more influence on the theological development of the worshipper than instrumental music does. The written word added to the musical setting combine to make it nearly impossible for the music not to have a profound impact on the theology of the worshipper. What the words say in the musical context become ingrained in the mind of those who sing them. Because of this, it is important to identify and understand the theological impact the different kinds of hymns and religious songs have on those who sing and hear them.

Because each person is a theologian in his own right, myriad theological understandings abound. These understandings run the gamut of possibilities as to what God is really like and how persons are to relate to that God. Part of the reason that there is such a variety of theological understandings is the nature of the hymns that have become meaningful to different persons in different religious groups.

Some songs and hymns concentrate solely on the nature and person of Jesus. Those who choose to sing them, nearly exclusively, eliminating others that deal with the nature of the Godhead or the Holy Spirit, develop a theology that is Christocentric. Their theology is unbalanced. It gives greater importance to the sacrifice of Jesus on the Cross than it does on the gift of "the Father's unfailing grace and forgiveness." "The blood of Jesus that washes away our sin" is emphasized more than our efforts to live righteous lives under the guidance of the Spirit. Those who concentrate only on the impact of

Jesus, almost eliminating the nature of the Creator and the power of the Holy Spirit, limit their view of God.

In like manner, some songs and hymns concentrate mainly on the mystery, might, and majesty of God the Creator. Those who choose to sing them nearly exclusively develop a theology that is Theocentric. Their theology also is unbalanced. It gives greater importance to the nature of the Divine-Force as being the creator of past history, present life, and future promise than it gives the gift of Jesus' sacrifice and his example for living through the power of the Spirit. Those who emphasize the creative force of God, almost eliminating the impact of Jesus, our example and redeemer, or the indwelling presence of the Spirit, limit their view of God, as well.

The same is true for those who emphasize the presence and power of the Holy Spirit. This theology is defined as Pneumocentric. Like those who hold a Christocentric or Theocentric theology, their theology is unbalanced. Their theology gives greater importance to the indwelling of the Spirit as a guide and companion through life than it places on the creative power of the Divine-Force or the example of Jesus and the redemption he offers.

Song and music not only channel our vision of the Triune God, they help to develop our theology on a practical level. The service music that is chosen provides the theological framework for our concept of the importance of the church in life. It sets the tone for a willingness to incorporate and involve others in our religious activities, signifying the importance of an ecumenical thrust for the work of the church. It enhances an understanding of the celebrations of the Christian year and the meaning of the rituals that are observed.

Songs and hymns that deal with the assurance of God's presence; the Incarnation (the presence of God in human form); the atonement Jesus provides on our behalf through the blood of Christ; his suffering on the Cross; and the Lordship, the name, and the example of Jesus; all help to round out a theological understanding of the relationship between the church and God.

There is one more group of songs and music, often included in worship around the time of some secular holidays that feeds our nationalistic pride and turns us from the worship of God. It is so subtle that unless our attention is called to it, we are apt to miss the movement entirely. Although the worship period is designed to honor God, oftentimes it is spent concentrating on the benefits enjoyed, living under the protection of civil authority. This move from the worship of God to nationalistic pride can be seen in others more easily than in our own actions. Think of the endless news reports, telling of the religious fervor of those who attempt to control the lives of others who do not believe as they do … all in the name of God. We can see the civil unrest within nations and between nations. Each side claims God is on their side. Each side calls upon God to bless their endeavors, and, as a result, the difference between God's will and the will of the nation becomes blurred.

The current struggles in the mid-East and between Euro-Soviet forces, as well forces in South-East Asia and in Central Africa that are being exerted upon our own nation today are examples. The conflict may center on purely religious issues, or it may focus on social or political issues, but no matter what the cause, when battle is waged and nationalistic pride is nurtured to the detriment or exclusion of theological concerns, humanity tends to rely more on our own selves than on God ... and terror and tyranny result.

It is a human tendency to believe God is on the side of the believer. Therefore, when any group of believers chooses to think that their blessings come from what they can provide for themselves, through their individual actions and their governmental structure, they have crossed the line from worshiping God to the worship of their way of life.

Around Independence Day, Memorial Day, Thanksgiving, and lesser civil holidays, nationalistic pride often trumps religious passion, dedication, and commitment to God. Certainly, much of our freedom is owed to some of the leaders of our nation. Honor should be given to the work they have done on our behalf. Contributions to civil betterment should be recognized. But none of this should replace the honor we give to God.

Often, country seems to take precedence over God, instead of the other way around. Calling ourselves a Christian nation doesn't make it so, unless our actions mirror the actions of the Christ to "love our neighbor as ourselves." Simply acknowledging God's influence upon our nation is not enough. Acknowledging God as the provider of all we enjoy as citizens of this nation enables us to be even better than we have been, for that act alone acknowledges that we are unworthy of the unbalanced earthly treasures enjoyed by this nation.

The goal of our nation's socio-economic policy is to better our citizen's well-being. Certainly, we enjoy the benefits of this policy. But that is not the subject here. The Christian is called to put others before self, and this causes myriad conflicts when trying to reconcile outside forces with theological understandings. It is important to acknowledge our nation's accomplishments and its shortcomings, and to call upon God to make us better.

Some of the most lustily sung songs in church are not those honoring God but those sung in praise of our nation. I raise this issue not to debase the value of what our nation offers, for it offers more than most. But, I propose one hymn in particular that recognizes the gifts our nation has provided, and at the same time it stands as a reminder that other nations do much the same for their citizens. Most of this hymn is a reminder of God's role in providing a taste of the freedom of life we want for all eternity. Is it not truer to our call to be witnesses and servants of God as we sing of the role God has in offering a better life to all whom God has created? The hymn, "This Is My Song" (Finlandia), provides a good example of how to keep things in perspective. The first two stanzas of the hymn were originally meant to stand on their own merit. The third verse was added to emphasize the importance of the hymn to Christians in particular. "This Is My Song" reflects more accurately the call the Divine-Force has on our lives than those songs we normally sing around our national holidays.

Rather than printing the lyrics of the first two stanzas by Lloyd Stone, you can hear for yourself the beauty of Finlandia by John Sibelius. Go to YouTube and pick from a wealth of videos featuring this hymn. If you are interested in the third stanza by Georgia Harkness, emphasizing the Christian interpretation of the hymn, you can find it in the current United Methodist Hymnal, #437. I am sure other denominations have this in their hymnal, as well.

It is hard for the American Christian to understand why so much of the world sees us as the enemy. It is nearly impossible to transition from the point of view commonly held in America that we are the protectors of freedom, to the view that some others hold that we are an imperialistic force that looks out only for our own well-being. But think of the phrase used so often by our politicians and government officials, "It is in our national interest." "It is in the interest of our nation" does not always equate with what is in God's interest for us. When we sing songs of nationalistic pride during worship, we must always be aware of our primary allegiance to God. We cannot allow our personal political perspective to determine how our Christianity will be expressed in the world. To do so is the beginning of the end of a theologically sound way of worship.

Next, in our consideration of the music emphasized in worship, we look at those hymns and songs that relate to death, heaven, and eternity. It helps to firm our concept of what life might be like in the presence of the Divine-Force after we pass from our earthly limitations onto an eternal existence. Each song we sing, hymn we share, and the music we hear helps to form our understanding of things that otherwise would be even more a mystery. Music helps to frame our faith in ways that are simple to experience, thereby making them powerful theological tools for faith development.

It is also important to recognize the impact that classical composers and their music have had on the Church. Through their music, the influence of Handel, Bach, Beethoven, and others have lifted the quality of worship to a magnitude worthy of an offering to God.

Other things influence our theological perspective. For instance, the way children are treated within the group reflects the group's understanding of the way God treats humanity. If children are treated as being less important than adults, this opens the door to belief that people who hold different views from the group are less important than dominant members of the group. Whenever a hierarchy of value is established for persons, there is a certainty that those who establish that hierarchy will be positioned at the top.

However, if children are viewed as being as important as adults, this opens the door to understanding that God values the potential of all persons as being ultimately important. It encourages the group to mentor each other and allows for the possibility that even the least powerful have a role in defining the group and the direction it takes. Children mirror the Christ-child entering the world in humble surroundings, powerless and defenseless ... traits carried by Jesus until his death on the Cross.

Being called "a child of God" is a title of respect and honor, if seen from the perspective of the Divine-Force. It is a title that lifts the possibility of great things, because it pictures the relationship between God and humanity. God is understood as being in control, and those whom God has created are understood to be witnesses of God's greatness and recipients of God's grace and love. As said in Isaiah 11:6, "... and a little child shall lead them."

If women are not allowed to hold leadership roles, then the group is deprived of the intellect, compassion, and understanding that is inherent in the feminine side of humanity. When we study the Creation stories of Genesis in the next chapter, this concept of humanity being complete only when both genders are considered full partners will be examined more fully. For now, it is enough to say that when half the population has limits imposed on them by the other half, much of what is good and beneficial and creative is lost for everyone.

The theology of any religious group is revealed when we look at whether secular activities and influences are incorporated into the life of the group. Some congregations choose not to allow, or at least limit as much as possible, the celebration rites of secular holidays and traditions even though many of those traditions have religious beginnings.

There is debate as to whether Halloween had Christian or pagan beginnings, but that is not of major importance for our discussion, because many Christian observances came about based on

the cycle of seasons. Remember, Christianity developed much like
other religions, and part of that development was based on the re-
curring climatic cycle and agriculture. The end of October marked
the time of harvest in the Northern hemisphere and the beginning
of the winter season. Pagan beliefs may have had an influence on
the beginnings of Halloween in that the gods of seed and harvest
were celebrated when the crops were gathered; or the Christian celebrations of "All Saints" (originally observed in May, but changed
to October by Pope Gregory IV) may have come about because of
Celtic or German influences. In any event, Halloween, or the "eve
of hallows," a holy event sanctioned by the Church, came to be celebrated with the wearing of costumes and going from door to door
to remind others of the souls who had passed on to purgatory but
had not reached the glory of heaven.

Today, congregations that resist the celebration of Halloween
believe that the holiday had come about because of pagan influences, and their resistance is a demonstration of the idea that it is
unholy to participate in those activities. It is a minority opinion in
that Halloween has become the second most financially profitable
holiday celebrated in America. It does not matter if Halloween had
its beginnings in pagan rites or in Christian celebrations. Halloween
has become a non-religious celebration for most persons. How and
whether individuals and congregations choose to observe it is a
demonstration of their theology. Some see it as a harmless venture
that has little religious significance. Others understand it as an obligation to maintain a vigilant stance about the importance of being
faithful in the face of secular challenge.

Two celebrations, having secular origins, Mother's Day and its complement, Father's Day, have been incorporated into the celebrations observed in many Christian congregations. Both these holidays represent the influence secular society has on religious practice. Persons within religious communities have recognized the importance of the relationship of motherhood and fatherhood to the well-being of the family unit and society in general. As a result, these secular celebrations have been adopted into the ritual of the congregation. Honoring mothers and fathers during worship by the giving of token gifts or simply by recognizing their status is a way of saying that the relationships we develop in the family have a positive influence on society in general and, therefore, mirror the hope of God for all relationships to be loving, nurturing, and compassionate. These two holidays are pure examples of the phenomenology of religion. Through them we are witnessing the transition of religious development in a simple but positive way.

Unfortunately, the way we celebrate some other holidays gives witness to how secularism can intrude on the religious development of the Church in general and individuals and congregations in particular. The two major Christian religious holidays are undergoing significant change. Christmas and Easter, the holidays commemorating the entrance of Jesus into the world and his departure from it, are changing from religious celebrations and becoming secular observances.

At Christmastime, some followers have chosen to draw the line against this secularization and have adopted the motto: "Jesus is the reason for the season." Their efforts reveal the struggle of many in religious communities to maintain the original impact of these holidays as being of great religious significance. Their struggle may be doomed to failure. Increasingly, Christmas is viewed as being a time for year-end economic growth. The media carries stories about the impact of retail sales on ending the year in the black. The socio-economic impact of Christmas on the world in general, and on America in particular, has fostered a revolution of thought both within and outside the Church. It seems almost unpatriotic to bemoan the trend that is taking place. This trend moves Christmas from the observance of God entering the world, so that the world might be saved from itself, to the idea that we can, through our own efforts, make life not just tolerable, but wondrous, through the exchange of goods and services.

In the short span of the last few generations, even the calendar has changed because of this movement. The traditional understanding was that the Christian year began with Advent (four weeks prior to Christmas), a time to prepare for the entrance of God into our lives. Next came Christmastide (a period of twelve days, commemorated by the song about "the partridge in a pear tree"). It was the time to celebrate the birth of the Christ-child and the stories of the shepherds coming to the manger. Epiphany followed (and lasted until Lent). It was the season that centered on the journey of the Wise Men to pay homage to Jesus. The point of Christmastide and Epiphany was to show that Jesus entered the world for everyone, from poor and humble to rich and powerful, including those of all nations, as represented by both the shepherds and the three kings. After Epiphany, the calendar moved on to Lent (a period of forty days, excluding Sundays). Lent was a time to examine our lives and seek forgiveness for our short-comings. Lent was followed by Easter, the celebration of God's unfailing nature to forgive and provide the world another chance. It celebrated the fact that humanity could become the creative force it was meant to be. The Sundays of this season emphasized the renewal of life possible through incorporating the spirit of Christ into our being. The last and longest season was Pentecost, the time of the church. It was a time of celebration for the way God could work through everyone to better the lives of others. Some religious groups have added a season or emphasized special days or a week or more of special significance, but for the most part, the Christian year cycles repeatedly, in the hope that humanity will finally get it right. The secularization of the church has disrupted the flow of that calendar.

Now, the year seems to begin with Christmas. The date of that beginning moves ever earlier in the year. The start of the Christian year is no longer set aside as a time of preparation for God's entrance into our lives, but emphasizes the buying of gifts for others and for ourselves. Now, when Christmas day arrives, Christmas ends. There is no longer the opportunity to continue the celebration of the birth of Christ for several days, as was the tradition in the past. Christmas has become an anti-climax, rather than an ever-expanding time for wonderment. The birth of Jesus is the only birth we celebrate by sending out announcements before the birth. The births of our own children are announced after the birth takes place. Doing so extends the joy of the moment to others we value. The sending of Christmas cards announcing the birth of Jesus (or even worse, emphasizing a secular message) takes away some of the celebration because it sets the scene for Christmas to be over, even before it starts.

Epiphany has lost its symbolism almost entirely. Instead of presenting the possibility that it is appropriate for God to be present in the lives of all persons in the world, the image has changed. The story of the Wise Men (representing those of other cultures) was originally told to show that all persons could gather on an equal basis to pay homage to the Christ-child. Their appearance was intended to be a parallel event to the story of the shepherds coming to the manger. The shepherds (representing the faithful to whom God was first revealed) originally were not considered to be the only ones to whom God would come. The story of the Wise Men was included to show that everyone, those of the faithful people and those of other backgrounds, could become a part of God's family. Those of the non-Christian world were included to have the opportunity to be a part of God's great plan. The inclusion of the Wise Men tells of the opportunity for everyone to bring gifts to God, just as faithful Christians are called to do. The gifts of the Magi were as special as the humble gift of the shepherds who had nothing to provide but their presence and their wonderment. The message of Epiphany is that all people are offered the chance to become a part of the family of God through Christ. Over the centuries, this message has been lost and Christmas has become more a means of separation, than a means of bringing the world together.

Like Christmas, Easter is being secularized and is becoming more of an economic engine. Its nature has not yet been changed to the extreme of Christmas, but it is undergoing pressures from outside the church. If or when Easter is changed to the extent that Christmas has changed, then the basis of the Christian faith is in danger of destruction. The theology of faithful believers is undergoing tremendous and insidious pressure. These thoughts go far beyond bemoaning change in tradition. They serve to call every faithful Christian to a renewal of theology.

We live in a dangerous time. Self-absorption has become a way of life. "Selfies" have become so commonplace that we hardly recognize what is happening to us. We send an unending flow of tweets and comments on other social media sites so that everyone can follow the simplest everyday activities of our lives. We carry cell phones as appendages so we can inform others we are in the snack aisle at the grocery store and then will be on our way to check out the pet supplies. The assumption is that others will be as enraptured with what we do as we are ourselves. This has happened in less than a decade.

Theologically, this is a problem because it sets up self as the center of the universe. We live in a time when it is easy to succumb to the temptation to serve ourselves over and above serving others and God, and this attitude subtly encroaches on everything we do … even our time of worship. Only God has the right to be God. Humanity is dependent on God's goodness and graciousness! Any theology that differs from this basic concept represents a dangerous turn in understanding. Honoring self over God takes from God the opportunity to help us fulfill our destiny to better the world and the lives of others. Honoring self is a non-starter. The Church teaches that each person is of value and has something to offer others. That mission is different from what society is practicing more and more each day. It is up to the church through its worship and teaching to bring our secular lives into balance with our religious life within the congregation.

The way rituals such as weddings, funerals, and baptisms are conducted all have a profound impact on the theology a person holds. Weddings can be a statement of the desire for God to be an integral part of the life of a new couple. It can be a statement of faith to announce to others the impact God is expected to have on the life of the family being created. A religious wedding ceremony is different from a civil union. It is more than something that meets the legal requirements of marriage. It establishes a different understanding of God's relationship to humanity. Even a religious wedding ceremony can be corrupted. When the main effort of a couple goes into the planning and execution of the wedding events rather than in celebrating the fact that a new family is being created in the name of God, something is wrong. Often, more effort is expended on the drama and production of the wedding than on preparations for making the marriage a lasting union. Many times, weddings lead to a breakdown in relationships rather than a strengthening of them.

In like fashion, a funeral offers an opportunity to publicly state the importance of God in the life of the one who had departed, and in lives of those who are affected by the death of another. A positive trend is a service that celebrates the life of the one who has died to commemorate the impact the departed has had on others. It recognizes the relationship one can have with others and with God. It helps to picture the inter-relationship one has with all of life and all who live. This kind of service goes beyond the traditional funeral that serves mainly to acknowledge our dependence on God.

The ritual of baptism makes a theological statement to the congregation. The baptism of an infant reveals that everyone is important to God, even those who cannot respond to God themselves, or even know about God. The act of baptism is an act of commitment when made by a person old enough and competent enough to fulfill that commitment to be faithful to God and the ways of God. Something else is being said when an infant is brought forth for baptism. The idea of commitment is maintained, but the commitment moves from the infant to those who surround the infant. Those persons take on the responsibility to fulfill the child's commitment to God until the child can do it for himself. Infant baptism reveals two things. The first is that God accepts us even if we are not capable of accepting God. The second is that others have the opportunity and the responsibility to work with God to make others aware of God's desire to be at one with us.

Like weddings and funerals, baptisms are to be public events. For a variety of reasons, adults often prefer that their baptism be done in private, as a rite between clergy and parishioner, and, many times, the rite is carried out in this manner. But in doing so, the minister places the personal preference for privacy over the spiritual meaning of the rite. Baptism is meant to be a community event, because it emphasizes the fact that we go through life connected to one another. No one can exist in a meaningful way on his own. To be fully human means that we are connected to each other and to God, and that connection is honored when baptism takes place in public. The one being baptized is making a statement to all that from that moment forward his life will be different because of his connection with God.

Baptism is a one-time ritual offered each person. Life changing events may make it seem that a re-baptism should be experienced. But re-baptism takes away the central meaning of the event. A binding contract was made. Neither God nor the person who was baptized has the option to "renegotiate" their commitment. Inherent in the promise made at baptism is the idea that God will honor the contract as offered; and God will help the person being baptized to maintain his part of the deal. Baptism is not like taking out an insurance policy that offers rewards so long as the premiums are paid. There is no magic offered through baptism. Baptism is not the key that unlocks the path to eternal life. There is no change in attitude on God's part about the worthiness of the person being baptized. Baptism is simply the public announcement of the fact that by being baptized we accept God's offer to love us and accept us and support us in our lives. Baptism is the sign that we accept the privilege of becoming a part of God's family and that we will do everything possible to be worthy of God's offer of love.

Consider, now, the architecture and design of places of worship and how those things affect theological understandings. Remember the story of Abougli in the first Chapter. The tribe came to the realization that God dwelt in the place where Abougli and the women had felt God's presence where they had stumbled and spilled the water they carried on their daily journey to provide the tribe with sustenance. The first thing they did was to build a shrine to God. They wanted to mark the place so all could see that God dwelt there.

Modern day people erect places to honor God's presence in their lives, too. The buildings they build reflect both their theology and the practical constraints that determine how "God's dwelling" will take shape. Historical events and tradition often reveal the foundation of their current theology. Economic forces, more recent family and community practices, and current needs reveal the more practical aspects of the expression of their faith through the churches they build. These driving forces do not always work together as a way that expresses their faith clearly. Because of this, it is appropriate to examine the constant struggle that exists between the effort to maintain tradition and time-honored ways to express faith with the very practical ways available to congregations who wish to be a witness to God in today's world.

Places of worship vary so greatly that a variety of theological messages are conveyed. Practical economic and geographic influences have something to do with the establishment of each location, but so do subtle theological understandings. Home centered places of worship, community buildings, and storefront centers may be sites of worship because of economic considerations … but they may be planned to reflect the concept that the place to meet God is the place where its members live and work. Simple surroundings may be as theologically appropriate as grand venues. Massive churches, seminary worship centers, cathedrals, and other such places of worship may have been built as a tribute to the grandeur of God or they may have been built as a way of gaining the respect of those of less influence or importance. These grand places of worship may have come about to signify the importance of those who chose to worship in such surroundings.

Those churches that dot the countryside and those churches that inhabit the neighborhoods of their membership may have come about as convenient places to gather and share a common background—or they may be raised to God's glory in the midst of the life they were given. No single theological understanding or practical reason can be attributed to the establishment of any place of worship. The same may be said about the choice of décor of any congregational gathering place. Rich tapestries and magnificent stained-glass windows are equally appropriate to stand alongside the simple wood hewn altar and plain white painted walls of the smallest of sanctuaries. What is important is that whatever style of building and whatever décor that is chosen reflect the sincere desire of the congregation to worship the Divine-Force of creation in a manner that is respectful and that encourages the idea that those who worship there are there because of their knowledge that God cares for them and wants them to reflect to all who pass by and pass through their doors the divine love they enjoy.

One last word about the worship experience needs to be addressed. Even though each participant is a theologian in his own right, it is the minister/priest who has been given the authority to set the tone, determine the style, deliver the homily (sermon) and decide the liturgy for worship. This authority may be granted by the church hierarchy or by the congregation, itself. In either case, the minister is there to guide her members to a deeper faith understanding. The minister needs to be sensitive to the needs and desires of her congregation. The minister is to decide if the comfort of the congregation is of primary concern, or if a more prophetic approach, challenging the congregation is needed.

It is important to be understanding of other Christian groups no matter the surrounding in which they worship. That concept reflects the idea that God accepts all who are called to be a part of God's family. That concept can be extended to the faithful of other religious groups. When the Divine-Force makes itself known in any surrounding, is not that place a place of God?

Premise of Chapter Eleven

How Scripture is interpreted defines the nature of God.

CHAPTER 11

"The Words and the WORD"

It was on a bitterly cold night and frosty morning, towards the end of the winter of '97, that I was awakened by a tugging at my shoulder. It was Holmes. The candle in his hand shone upon his eager, stooping face, and told me at a glance that something was amiss.

'Come, Watson, come!' he cried.
'The game is afoot. Not a word!
Into your clothes and come!'

Doyle, Arthur Conan, Sir. <u>The Return of Sherlock Holmes</u>, "The Adventure of the Abbey Grange." 1904. (New York: McClure, Phillips & Co. 1905.)

LIFE IS A mystery. Much of our time is spent trying to find answers to that mystery. There is more to living than the daily humdrum of existence. As human beings, we exist in a realm that has parameters different from the arena of life for other living creatures. This difference lies in the fact that we seek answers to the goings on around us. At times it may seem we are like inhabitants of an ant colony … each ant having a single purpose for life, searching and finding food for existence; working to redo collapsed tunnels for movement; digging deeper to avoid the scorching sun or flooding rains; fighting other life forms that intrude on the colony, defending by bite and poison; and reproducing simply because the call of life is to go on living. As human beings, we do all those things the ant does, but we are different. That difference lies in the fact that we seek answers to the mysteries that confront us, and we do it in a variety of ways. We try to understand, something quite different from trying to exist.

Some turn to science to discover the secrets of life, following applied methods and controlled structure. Others turn to less defined methods that attempt to explain the "why" of human thoughts and actions. Life not only presents a mystery for us to unravel, but also the drive to unravel that mystery. As the creation of God, we find ourselves in the role of detective so we can discover the underlying causes of our situation and solve the mystery of how to go on living in new and more complete ways. We all belong to the society of investigators headed by the famous mythical detective, Sherlock Holmes.

No matter what our religious persuasion, we are to search for the meaning that lies beneath the surface of our relationships. In this chapter, we will look especially at one of the tools the Christian uses in making that search. Earlier in the book, the Wesleyan Quadrilateral was presented. We found that John Wesley used four sources to develop his theology: Scripture, Tradition, Experience, and Reason. This chapter relates to the first arm of Wesley's Quadrilateral. It deals with the importance of having a scriptural base that helps form our theology and provides some of the answers we seek about life.

The Bible is a bestseller. It sits on the shelves of libraries, in the homes of Christians and persons of other faiths, and those who claim no religious connection at all. It has claimed a place of importance in the history of humankind. Despite this, the modern-day reader holds a basic misconception about the Bible. The misconception is not about the faith development possibilities of its content. The misconception is about the book, itself. It is at this point that the Bible must be examined through the eyes of a detective.

The Bible may sit on a shelf with books detailing modern accounts of historical events. It may sit beside books that analyze the important features of how the Bible helps to develop the faith of persons. It has a place near books on philosophy and psychology and sociology. It complements books of science and technology. But the Bible is different from all these other books because it is a book of ancient, oriental literature. It cannot be read with understanding only from the modern point of view. It must consider the views and understandings of the people for whom it was first written.

"There are three ways of reading the Bible, and these three ways must have interplay with each other to understand what it has to say to us today." [NOTE: Robt. L. Browning, Chas. R. Foster, Everett Tilson, "Ways the Bible Comes Alive in Communicating the Faith," Nashville. Abdingdon Audio-graphics. 1975.].

First, the content of the Bible was written for those who lived at the time the words were written. Its content was meant to explain how God could work in their lives, which is not the same as the way God can work in the lives of those living today. Reading the Bible without some basic understanding of the events being described and the impact those events had on humanity leaves the reader without some of the clues necessary for applying it to today's situations. Daily life in biblical times was different not just in the hardships endured without the advances that have been made through science and technology, but also because of the changes that have occurred in civil society. Rewards and punishments were not the same as what is experienced today. Style of government has changed. The economic system of biblical times was unlike the system we have today. The importance of the family unit and the value of the individual were determined by birth order, gender, physical strength, and the status the individual's family had in society. The average life span of those of biblical times was much shorter than it is now. The freedoms enjoyed were unlike today's freedoms. The relationships between friends and neighbors were of a different nature than what modern people have with those they consider important. Life in biblical times had little in common with life today. When the Bible is read taking all these things into consideration, it allows us to form new understandings. What was being said to those of biblical times was being said to a people who were very different from us.

Second, we need to consider the fact that the people to whom the words were written were of an oriental culture. In our society, when someone speaks of those who are Asian, they are usually referring to those of Chinese or Korean or Japanese descent. But the Bible was written for those who lived in what we now call the mid-East, an area around the Mediterranean Sea. A detective would take that into consideration, because those who lived in that area reflected diverse cultural influences from those living on the European continent. People of European descent experienced pressures and influences that were unlike those experienced by persons who were Asian. This recognizes that the geography and climate; the time period in which the two cultures developed; the peoples who impacted the two cultures; and the civil, social, and religious dissimilarities between them all have made a difference in what the modern-day Christian, especially the American Christian, has as his outlook and understanding of life. Until that is understood, there is the likely possibility that the content and the context of biblical interpretation will be a problem.

Finally, because the Bible is literature, it reflects two things. First, its content reveals the attitudes, ideas, ideals, and values of the writers who contributed to the words that were chosen. Literature cannot be separated from the essence of the author. What appears in black and white (and red, if you have a Bible translation that claims to have the words of Jesus recorded verbatim) is shaded by the understandings and bias of the authors. Literature is not the same thing as a transcript of a courtroom exchange between lawyer and witness where a judge rules what can be included and what must be omitted. The books of the Bible, as literature, are subject to the understandings and interpretations and the bias of those who wrote the words that we read.

The Bible, as literature, is subject to the understandings and interpretations and the bias of the reader, as well. No one can confront the Bible simply as if his mind were like an empty vessel ready to be filled with the truth. Anything that goes into the vessel of our mind is filtered by experience and the power of reason; and what results is an interpretation that reflects the personal bias of the reader. We say that the writers of the Bible were inspired to write the words we read. No doubt, this is true. But it is true also that the reader is inspired to take from those words things that seem to round out previously held beliefs and understandings, as well as an occasional new inspirational insight.

The Bible is the inspired word of God because of the way both the authors and the readers of its content interpret its meaning—not because God ordained the words that have been written, a concept held by the early Church to enforce its impact on a less sophisticated audience. The Bible is ancient, oriental literature, which means it must be seen from the perspective of those for whom it was first written. [NOTE: For a more complete discussion of the Bible seen as ancient Oriental literature, I recommend The Layman's Bible Commentary, volume one, Introduction to the Bible. It provides help, putting Holy Scripture in perspective, so that we can get the most out of it. No longer in print, it is available in many libraries and e-libraries.].

We are to read the Bible from the perspective of its original audience. It is important also to try to read it from God's perspective. We must trust that God has given us the intellect and the insight to discern some basic truths of life. The Divine-force of creation has provided the means to examine and interpret our relationships and experiences, so they shed light on what seems right or wrong, good or bad, truth or falsehood.

With these interpretations, the stories and examples of the Bible can take on personal meaning as we attempt to prepare ourselves for lives that reflect our best hopes and what we believe God hopes for us. This way of reading the Bible is not as easy as reading it from the perspective of our religious ancestors, but it is equally important. This approach allows us to theologize. Reading the words from what we imagine to be God's perspective changes the Bible from an accounting of history and a collection of faith stories to a revelation of who and what God is like. The Bible becomes a means of determining the nature of God. Even though we say we are created in the image of God, we go about life creating God in the image we believe to be true. Scripture, like tradition, reason, and experience, allows us to do just that.

Most people read the Bible, asking, "What does this passage or story mean to me, personally?" "How does its message give guidance to my life?" In one sense, this approach seems to be the most valuable way to read the Bible. We use the words we read to guide us in concrete ways to a richer life. What could be better?

Because, generally, the outcome of reading the Bible in this manner has positive results, it is hard to argue its value. But the Bible has much more to offer than being a guidebook for life. If it is reduced to a "how to" manual for living, much of its value is lost. It is important to see how we've become an extension of "God's People" through the centuries. It is important to understand that we have an historic place in the furthering of God's kingdom. And it is important to believe there is more for us to experience beyond our temporal existence. If the Bible is used only as a guidebook for living, we lose the rest of its value.

Reading the Bible with the eye of a detective requires effort, but in doing so there is a reward at the end of the case. The rest of this chapter will provide a few examples of how reading the Bible in the ways just described can be accomplished.

First, look at the creation stories in Genesis. They have two messages, and they present themselves in two distinct ways, having different styles. They give us clues to what God's people were like in two different time periods, and this gives us a better understanding as to how God relates to people based on their distinct ways of life.

These accounts appear in the first few chapters of Genesis. The one starting at the first verse of chapter one is really the second account of Creation. This seems counter-intuitive because it reads like an introduction to the whole Bible. It starts with the words, "In the beginning ... God." But, for our purpose, we start with some of the clues in the second story, the one that begins in chapter two. It is the story of Adam and Eve.

Remember Genesis is not just Christian scripture; it, along with the next four books of the Bible, Exodus, Leviticus, Numbers, and Deuteronomy, were taken from Jewish scripture. The collection of these writings is known as the Pentateuch. The story of Adam and Eve is a simple tale. Long before there was an organized Jewish faith, the people needed a way to learn about God and how they could relate to God. So, they told about their faith in story form. By doing that even children could remember how God operated in their lives.

Those early believers were much like the plantation slaves in our country. Most of them could neither read nor write, so they had no books and couldn't worship as we do today. They needed a way to tell each other about their faith and about their God. So, they told stories to each other, and they sang songs about their lives. In movies about slavery some deep-throated voice would sing, "Nobody knows the trouble I've seen, nobody knows my sorrow." [NOTE: From the Negro spiritual of the same name, attributed to several arrangers through the years. Lyrics and music were altered to adapt to the style of many performers.] And, then a chorus of voices would join in, and they all sang as they worked ... not out of joy, but out of a shared experience. The songs and stories of these slaves told of their lives, what God was like, and how they could relate to God.

Imagine how the story of Adam and Eve might have been told to early people eons ago. They, like the plantation slaves, were tired, worn out by a hard day's labor with no personal reward. Picture yourself among them, sitting on the ground or on a rock in the yard of the oldest person in the tribe. You had gathered with all the others for a chance to tell of the happenings of your day. You had no television or radio or internet to entertain yourself. There were no books to read. The only entertainment you had was conversation with each other. You had a tough day toiling in the sun. The ground wasn't very fertile, and what crops you grew were meager. After the initial conversation about the happenings of the day began to subside, quiet descended on the group. This day had been pretty much like all the other days that had gone before. Hot sun, hard work, little reward, sore muscles, and parched throats were all you could talk about. Then, someone asked the elder of the tribe to tell one of his stories. We use the text of the story from the third chapter in Genesis as the words the elder would have used. [NOTE: As in earlier biblical references, the New Revised Standard Version of the Bible is used.]

The elder begins the story much like a camp counselor might begin a scary tale around the campfire. He starts in the middle of the story this time, for they all knew it from beginning to end (Genesis 3:1-7). He's talking about the villain of the story, so his voice is low, almost a whisper.

"Now the serpent was more crafty than any other creature the Lord God had made. The serpent said to the woman, 'Did God say, "You shall not eat from <u>any</u> tree in the garden"?

The serpent is asking something for which he already has the answer. It's a way to get the woman to say what he wants her to say, because he's setting a trap for her.

"The woman said to the serpent, 'Oh no, we may eat of the fruit of the trees in the garden; but God said, 'You shall not eat of the fruit of the tree that is in the middle of the garden, nor shall you touch it, or you shall die.'"

The members of the tribe know that the woman has fallen into the trap. The serpent got her to repeat what God had told her, so now, he can put forth his argument to convince the woman that he knew better than God what she should do.

His next words were uttered with contempt and sounded almost incredulous, as if he couldn't believe what the woman had said. It's as if he had said: "Oh, for crying out loud, you don't really believe that line God gave you, do you?" The serpent said to the woman, "You shall not die; for God knows that when you eat of it your eyes will be opened, and you will be like God, knowing good and evil."

The elder of the tribe knew he got the story right, because like the woman in the story, he and all his listeners had experienced the desire to be wiser than they were. They wanted to have all the answers, so that their lives would be easier and they could avoid all the troubles they had.

This is the story of every human being. Everyone wants to be more like God. We want to know right from wrong, not just to avoid the wrong, but to be able to use that knowledge to fill our appetite for good living. It is part of human nature to want more than we have, to be more than we are.

The elder tells how the woman rationalized what the serpent had said. She wanted to believe that she could be more like God. "So, when the woman saw that the tree was good for food, and that it was a delight to the eyes, and that the tree was desired to make one wise, she took of its fruit and ate; and she also gave some to her husband, who was with her, and he ate. Then the eyes of both of them were opened, and they knew that they were naked; and they sewed fig leaves together and made loin cloths for themselves."

At this point in the story, unless we read it with the eyes of a detective, we are apt to miss an important point. The serpent may have been crafty and the villain of the story, but the serpent did not lie to the woman. The serpent got his way by telling the truth. When Eve and Adam ate the forbidden fruit, they became wiser. They understood more fully the difference between right and wrong. They became more like God.

This tale is an allegory of the way humanity experiences life. The human condition makes us vulnerable to a host of forces. Sometimes even the truth can lead us down the wrong path. We can never be fully certain that the way we travel is the righteous way—and that is a hard thing for someone Christian to believe. The typical Christian reasons, if he does his best to follow the teachings of Jesus and make what seems the "Christian" choice, why can he not be certain that he is doing God's will? The answer lies in the fact that no single decision or action can ever stand alone. Everything we do is interrelated with everything others do. Everything we are is associated with everyone else. We cannot control the outcome, even if we believe we are as wise as God. In this sense, the serpent lied to the woman. He lied by omission. The serpent chose not to let the woman know all the ramifications that could result from being more like God. Every day we pay the price of falling for the words of the "crafty" serpent. But is the serpent the only one to blame?

Of course not! Just look at the story (Genesis 3:8-19). It continues with God walking through the Garden. God is intent on confronting Adam and Eve with the choices they have made. We need to move into detective mode again. We find God searching for the two "perps," who have broken the law by eating of the fruit from the Tree of Knowledge of Good and Evil. God calls out to Adam. "Where are you?"

God already knows where Adam is. But this is the story of God's continual search for us and the story of God's willingness to allow us to respond as we choose. These three words reveal the way God's image has been created by each person who hears the story. The words God speaks reveal how the one listening to the story understands God. If these words sound harsh and seem to be uttered in anger, then the image one has of God is an image of a vindictive God, who is just waiting for us to "slip up" and reveal our weaker side. The God image we create does something else, too. It defines God in terms to which we can relate, and it also provides the parameters that we use to define our own lives. It sets up an artificial "universe" in which we exist. The God-image we create defines the options we have, to live out our lives. So, what we do with these images is vitally important.

There are several ways to interpret the words God called out in the search for Adam and Eve. The words, "Where are you?" may have been uttered harshly and in anger ... but probably not. It is hard to justify the image of an angry God with the claim that "God is Love" or that "God is a forgiving God" or that "God is a God who offers acceptance."

As detectives, can we find another possibility for the way God called out? It seems truer to the nature of God as being loving and forgiving and accepting to hear God calling out the way a worried mother might call out, as she searches for her children who had left the safety of their backyard to venture into the harsh surroundings of an unknown world.

Think of the way a loving mother would call out, not letting her worry seep into her voice, lest her children become afraid. Think of the playful lilt of her voice, rising and falling, calling out the words, "Where are you?" as if she were playing hide-and-seek, all the time knowing where her children were … hiding behind a bush or under the bed or behind the living room curtains. As detectives, does this not seem more consistent with the way we claim God to be?

If we believe God to be loving and accepting, this image of God as a searching parent seems more appropriate than an image of God who searches us out to wreak punishment. If God is omnipotent and omniscient, then God wouldn't have had to search for Adam and Eve. But the story tells us that God did search. So there had to be a reason. The reason was that God still wanted to have a loving relationship with Adam and Eve, so the search was made not to find them, but to open the door for them to communicate.

The elder goes on with his story. God continues searching and when Adam and Eve are found, what does God do? Even a detective might be surprised. Instead of the way many would expect God to act, the elder tells his listeners that God doesn't get all tied up in righteous indignation and blast the two for their actions. No, the elder tells that God quietly confronts Adam first, asking him what he has done. God gives Adam the chance to confess and take whatever punishment is to come "like a man." There is no lightning bolt shot out of the blue, just the question, "What is it that you have done?"

Adam responds, defending himself, for he knows he has been disobedient. All Adam must do to know that God loves him is to look around and see all the wonder and beauty God has provided. God has already told him that the Garden is his to enjoy (Genesis 2:4b-25). Everything God has made is given to him—everything, that is, except the tree that grows in the middle of the Garden, the Tree of the Knowledge of Good and Evil. And Adam has violated this one simple rule ... leave that tree alone, for as the serpent said, "If you touch that tree, you will become like God."

So, Adam responds. He tells God that he realized that he was naked and he was afraid (a subtle admission that he had disobeyed the restriction God had set not to touch the Tree of the Knowledge of Good and Evil); but he does not actually admit his guilt. He answers with an excuse, as if he could convince God that there were "mitigating" circumstances. He maintains that he really wasn't to blame. He responded like a petty thief caught with the spoils of his crime. He tries to put the blame on Eve. Adam even goes further and tries to blame God, as well. "It was the WOMAN, the one YOU gave me." "She took of the fruit and ate, and she gave me some and I ate." Detectives hear it all the time when the subject whines his excuse. "You gotta understand. I didn't mean it. It wasn't me who thought all this up. I was just doing what I was told."

Still, God doesn't get angry. All God does is to turn to Eve for confirmation. What does Eve do? Like Adam, Eve tries to shift the blame. She places the fault on the serpent. "The serpent tricked me, and I ate." It was a simple defense, but inadequate.

A clever detective would note that there was a difference in the way God dealt with Adam and Eve from the way the serpent was treated. Both Adam and Eve were given a chance to confess their transgression and to explain their actions, but the serpent was not given that opportunity. Some might say it was because the evidence was too compelling against the serpent ... both Adam and Eve blamed the whole thing on the serpent. However, would their word be enough to change God's whole approach?

If God is understood to be loving and forgiving, One who placed more value on humankind than on anything else, then the way God was pictured as dealing with Adam and Eve had to be different from the way with which the serpent was dealt. Both Adam and Eve were given the chance to explain themselves. But the serpent had no such chance. Instead, God chose to punish the serpent more like a vindictive God might do. God starts out, telling the serpent, "Because you have done this, cursed are you among all animals and among all creatures; on your belly you shall go, and dust you shall eat..." There was no second chance for the serpent. What was done was done.

Adam and Eve experienced repercussions for their disobedience, but they weren't punishments that changed their very nature. Instead, the suffering they were to endure explained the things the Elder and his tribe experienced in daily life. The woman would be attracted to the man even though their union would ultimately bring pain in childbirth. The gift of being able to provide life and the chance to nurture that life was still to be enjoyed by the woman. The man was no longer able to enjoy the Garden without having to toil for food. He was not cursed; the ground was cursed. He was going to have to work for his keep. The story of these two explained why life was like it was for the people who first heard it. After Adam was told his fate, those who heard the story were reminded that they were not like God ... "you are dust, and to dust you shall return."

The story goes on (Genesis 3:20-24). A good detective would know that if the story ended here, God would have been pictured as being a vengeful God, one to be feared anytime a person failed to meet God's expectations. But the story continues to reveal God's forgiving nature. The man is allowed to name his wife, just as he had named all the creatures God had made. Her name was Eve. The name carried the meaning "to breathe," "to live," or "to give life." Her name indicated she had a purpose. She was to be the progenitor of the human race and, especially, the mother of God's family. The man and the woman were still trusted enough to fulfill the mission of fostering God's family.

The elder's story pictures God as providing the essential things the man and the woman needed for their lives, even though they had failed to live up to God's hope for them. They were punished, but they were also protected. The man and the woman had disobeyed God and ate the fruit from the Tree of Knowledge of Good and Evil, so God wanted to be sure they no longer had the opportunity to eat from the Tree of Life, as well. They had to leave the blissful life of the Garden because if they stayed there and ate from the Tree of Life, they would live forever, like God. After all, the wise elder knew that God was God, and the man and woman were limited by their humanity.

God fashioned clothing for the man and the woman because they could no longer remain in the Garden. They needed protection from the elements, and they were aware of their nakedness. The gift of clothing was symbolic of God's everlasting love for them, even though they had to live under the terms of God's punishment. To ensure they would not come back and try to eat from the Tree of Life, a sentinel was positioned at the entrance of the Garden to keep the man and the woman out. God and humanity had different places in the scheme of things from that point on. It was no longer to be life in the Garden, but it was still to be life in God's family.

By now, everyone, who had gathered to hear the elder's story, was very sleepy. It was dark, and in a few short hours everyone would be roused to face another day of hard work. Even though their lives were hard, the story the elder told gave them hope and they realized once again that they were a part of God's family and that God loved them.

Remember, one of the tools a good detective uses is the search for similar events that may shed light on the case. Fortunately, the story of Adam and Eve has a corollary account of Creation in Genesis. This account is the one that appears first (Genesis 1:1-31). This new account seems to be in its rightful place, because it conveys the idea that it is an account of the beginning of the creation. But its style and content belies the idea that it was the first account of Creation.

Its style and tone yield several clues to prove the idea that it is a much later version of the story of Creation. It has a different purpose for being included in the Bible. There are many signs that support this theory and we will consider a few of them.

Even the most cursory reading of the two stories of Creation reveals that they have different styles. The one already examined is a simple tale. It came from a time when those hearing and telling it could witness to their faith and answer some very basic questions confronting them in life.

This new account appears in a form that is much closer to other things we read today. There is no story form to it. It conveys its message in a logical way, and lends itself to the written word. By the time it was written, those who valued its content were already a part of a faithful community. It reveals some of the important ideas that existed in that early faith community.

The first words of the text, "In the beginning ... God" set the stage to remind the faithful that before anything else, God existed. God was and is the prime mover in history. It conveyed the subtle idea that even though humanity strives to be like God, humanity is playing a catch-up game. The writers of these few words had learned the lesson the elder had taught when he told his story to those who had labored in the fields. By now they had learned that it was God who was in control, and it was God who set the standards for faithful living.

This story was written to a much later group of persons, answering the questions with which these persons were struggling. It provided a means of seeing God in personal terms, yet it established the fact that God was orderly and in control, even though their world seemed chaotic. The story was meant to bring comfort to those who lived in a society of long ago, as they faced different issues from those who related to the story of Adam and Eve.

It was not meant to answer questions that people from our day ask. Questions like, "How could God exist even before the universe existed?" "How long was a day of Creation?" "Did humankind evolve?" Such questions are not answered in this passage. It isn't an historical account ... it is an allegory that persons used to gain understanding for their time. Other biblical stories and passages must be used to answer the questions of the 21st century, for they extend and expand our knowledge of God and of life itself. They round out the rudimentary understandings this chapter of Genesis brings.

Look at the account of Genesis 1. Those who attend church services regularly, or who may attend just an occasional wedding or funeral, may see some similarity in the way this story is presented. This passage is a Responsive Reading. Our examination begins in the middle of the reading.

The leader starts.

(Genesis 1:11) Then God said, "Let the earth put forth vegetation: plants yielding seed and fruit trees of every kind on earth that bear fruit with its seed in it."

Then the people respond.

AND IT WAS SO.

The leader goes on.

(Genesis 1:12) The earth brought forth vegetation: plants yielding seed of every kind bearing fruit with its seed in it.

Then the people respond.

(Genesis 1:13) AND GOD SAW THAT IT WAS GOOD. AND THERE WAS EVENING AND THERE WAS MORNING, THE THIRD DAY.

The leader continues.

(Genesis 1:14) And God said, "Let there be lights in the dome of the sky to separate the day from the night; and let them be for signs and for seasons and for days and years, and let them be lights in the dome of the sky to give light upon the earth."

Then the people respond.

AND IT WAS SO.

The leader takes his turn.

(Genesis 1:16) God made the two great lights—the greater light to rule the day and the lesser light to rule the night—and the stars. God set them in the dome of the sky to give light, upon the earth, to rule over the day and the night, and to separate the light from the darkness.

Again, the people respond.

(Genesis 1:18b) AND GOD SAW THAT IT WAS GOOD. AND THERE WAS EVENING AND THERE WAS MORNING, THE FOURTH DAY.

All religions develop in a similar way. First, a group of people begins to understand that a mysterious Power exists that affects their group. This Power is external and lies beyond their control. Because this Power transcends their ability to control their lives, they pay homage to it. Over time, this Power is personalized. It reflects their sense of being and takes on human characteristics without being hampered by human limitations. This pattern is true for small indigenous groups and for large world religions.

The first chapter of Genesis was written when the people of Israel had developed their religious understandings enough to need order and organization for their faith. Their religion had gained a strong enough foothold to be a defining feature of who they were. The story of Creation most certainly came from the liturgy of an early Jewish worship service. The needs of society dictated that moral and ethical guidance was needed to strengthen the cultural needs of its people. The development of religion was not just an altruistic way of molding the religious thinking of society's members. It did more. It lifted the moral and ethical thinking of persons, but it also helped in the formation of religion itself. The words that follow below don't just tell of God and Creation. They tell also of the need of organized religion to extend its influence over the faithful. A clear example of this is seen in Genesis 2:1-3.

Thus, the heavens and the earth were finished, and all their multitude. And on the seventh day God finished the work that he had done, and he rested on the seventh day from all the work that he had done. So, God blessed the seventh and hallowed it, because on it God rested from all the work that he had done in creation.

Before looking at this story of Creation from the three perspectives we are to use to read the Bible, it is important to note a subtle idea here. It must be asked if the persons who included this passage had an ulterior motive for its inclusion. People in biblical times were basically the same as the people who live now, except for the changes society has imposed, making them adapt to the forces they encountered. No sane person has ever done anything without having some reason for it. Why was this passage included as the summary of God's activity of Creation?

We must assume that those responsible for the words that were written were written by the religious leaders of the day. They were the theologians, the pastors, and the worship leaders of this developing faith group. What did these religious leaders have to gain from the message of this passage?

It is important to remember that whenever a religious group gets to the point in its development to have a coordinating body to maintain control over the group, one of the responsibilities of this coordinating group is to strengthen and perpetuate the group, itself. Religious leaders become administrators. There would be nothing more important to this group of administrators than to find a way to maintain control over the members of their organization. They had to assure the importance of their position in the eyes of those who followed them. What better way was there than to set aside a time when their presence and influence was guaranteed? If after six days, the seventh day was reserved for rest and the observance of God's labor on behalf of their membership, these administrators were guaranteed a secure position within the group. Today, it is called "job security." That may seem cynical, but that is the way human beings operate.

The benefit gained by the group is that it provides a time reserved for recognizing God's importance in the cycle of life. Still, it is important to recognize that even the church is subject to the same pressures other groups in secular society must face. The church is not exempt from having to justify its importance and relevance in society.

It is important to read the Bible from three different points of view.

First, in this story of Creation, the people needed to learn that God had provided an order to the universe, thereby giving them freedom from understanding the universe as a random and chaotic environment. They needed to know that they could have a better understanding of their surroundings and thereby have more control over their lives. The people had moved beyond the simple need of hearing stories of God's interplay with humans. They had progressed to the point of understanding some basic principles of astronomy and the movement of the universe. They were more in control of agronomy and animal husbandry, but they needed that control to be tempered by the understanding they had of God's desire for their lives.

Second, this account of Creation, as seen from God's point of view, dealt with the faithful in more specific ways than in the story of Adam and Eve. The people were not viewed as being subject to the whims of nature and the need to eke out their livelihood. They were beginning to see themselves as partners with God.

Third, the idea that there was a one-time act of creation has ended. A new concept of creation is now offered and it opens the story to understanding it from a present-day point of view. Humankind along with God can now be understood as being partners in the ongoing process of creation in all aspects of life. In this story of Creation, God relinquishes the power of control over our environment to those living today. It is a great freedom <u>and</u> a great responsibility. With this idea comes the understanding that God is not going to do for us what we should do for ourselves. One of the keys of this story is that God has given us dominion over creation. For those living today, this story means we no longer can step back and simply ask God to straighten out the mess we make of our lives and our relationships.

"What God gives, God can take away" is bad theology, as seen considering this story of Creation. The gifts that God gives are freedom, love, acceptance, hope, the idea that our lives are intricately interwoven with the lives of others, the promise that we will not be forgotten, the responsibility to live obeying our best instincts, and the strength to be an ongoing force of Creation. These things will not be taken away.

God does not hand out favors to the faithful and the righteous, while withholding blessings from those who care only for themselves. Nothing we do can merit God's love ... it is already ours. We ask, "Why do bad things happen to good people?" and "Why do good things happen to bad people?" The answer is simple ... it is a part of life. God does not reward or punish us for the way we live. Yes, sometimes the consequences for our actions catch up with us, but that is not God's doing; and yes, sometimes it seems we are rewarded for the good we do, but that comes from others, not God. Living outside the Garden means we are subject to all manner of forces. If we do good things to bend God's will in our favor, then we miss the point of God being willing to share the power of Creation with us. That is as bad as trying to rationalize away the impact of doing bad things, which hurt the lives of others.

God's work is not finished! We are not left alone! The creative force of God continues to move throughout the world in and through us. As a part of God's family, we are partners in the divine work of creation. Though we no longer live in the Garden, God calls us to make a garden out of the place where we live.

Epilogue

I KNOW YOUR religious understandings, especially your vision of God, is very personal. It can be upsetting when anyone offers a different viewpoint. My intent has not been to upset but simply to offer new possibilities for growth in your religious life. Whether you agree with some of the thoughts I have expressed, or whether you mostly disagree, is not the point. The purpose of this book is not to convince you to adopt my personal theology. God has given you a heart, mind and soul, and the freedom to make your own choices about what it is you believe. My purpose is to help you understand why you believe what you believe and to encourage you to examine those beliefs for yourself.

Whether you like it or not, you are a theologian. Most of us shy away from that understanding, believing that theology is something best reserved for the "experts." But, if you have any concept of what God is like and how God wants you to live out your life with the rest of humanity, you are theologizing.

The image of God and the understanding of the role we play in the Kingdom of God has changed through history. This has happened for many reasons. It is crucial that the religious concepts of any society fit into the needs of that society. But, that does not mean the image of God can deviate so drastically that the very essence of God is altered. The nature of God is constant. How we interpret God's nature can be different for each person, but that interpretation is different from the reality of God. God cannot be loving, forgiving and gracious while at the same time be vindictive, malicious and capricious. Each person's image of God must be consistent, or we fall into a trap we cannot escape. The one rule all of us must follow, as we try to picture God and God's call upon us, is that we must end up with a picture that is unchanging for all situations and in all relationships. Unless this happens, there is more work to do.

Do not misunderstand me. Developing a valid theology, one that is consistent, is hard work! We covered some of the reasons people of faith settle for half-developed theologies. The most common reason is that we settle for a theology that makes us comfortable even though that theology is not fully worked out and, therefore, cannot fully comfort us in times of need or as we attempt to be God's agents of love to a hurting world. So, this is your invitation to get back to work. It is now up to YOU to *Find the Fingerprints of God in the Twenty-First Century*. You are welcome to use this book as your guide.

Thank you for joining me on this adventure of faith.

About the Author

J. Allen Thompson is an ordained United Methodist minister who received his MDiv and MACE from the Methodist Theological School in Ohio. He also studied at the Pontifical College Josephinum in Columbus, Ohio—the only Roman Catholic seminary in North America administered by the US Council of Bishops under the auspices of the Vatican. He pastored congregations in Ohio and Illinois, and he served as a chaplain at the Methodist Medical Center in Peoria, Illinois. He and his wife, Maggie, have a blended family of five children and nine grandchildren.

Author Contact Information

ONE OF THE underlying themes of this book is that we are all theologians in our own right. Because of this, I welcome all critiques you may have.

Remember, this book is not intended to persuade you to believe the things I have included. The purpose I had in writing is to expand your knowledge by getting you to think about what it is you believe.

You can accept it and grow, or you can reject it and become more firmly rooted in your present beliefs. When that happens, you will grow as well. I ask only that you read, digest and analyze the information I have included, and then evaluate it so that you can help me grow in my own understandings, too.

You can contact me on my website at: http://focusontheology.com/. Or, by email at:FocusOnTheology@gmail.com.

Peace,
J. Allen Thompson